Narc·tion·ar·y

The Narcissistic Abuse
Recovery Dictionary

A WORLD OF ITS OWN
HAS A LANGUAGE OF ITS OWN

DR. TRACY ®, PH.D.

To my Momsie···
Who taught me how to slay ghosts.

Table of Contents

arguing in bad faith
assigning responsibility
assigning status
awakening

B _____ **44**

baiting
bait and switch
battles without resolution
belief conflicts
belief system
benign return
bidding
big / bigger syndrome
birthrights
black-and-white thinking
black cloud syndrome
blame shifting
body language abuse
boiling frog syndrome
boundary
boundary push(es)
boundary push-backs
brainwashing
branding
broken heart syndrome
broken record syndrome
bubble living
burdening
burnout

C — 54

D — 65

defining reality
defining truth
deflecting
delusional narcissist
de-masking
denial
detectiving
devaluation phase
diminished identity
director of judgement
discard
dissociation
dissociative amnesia
distancing
divide and conquer
dog whistling
domestic violence
domination
do-over
dosing
double binding
double standards
drama triangle
drilling for fuel
dsm

E   76

ego-syntonic
emotional abuse
emotional bandwidth
emotional blackmail
emotional boundaries
emotional dissonance

emotional face blindness
emotional flashback
emotional home base
emotional homelessness
emotional infection
emotional manipulation
emotional neglect
emotional neutral
emotional terrorist
emotional terrorism
emotional thinking
emotional threshold
emotional vampire
empath
empathy deficient
empty husk
enabler
engaging
enmeshment
episodic
erased syndrome
explosive disorder
ex-recycling

F   86

fake empathy
false flattery
false self
fauxpology
fear bombing
fearland
fictional character
final discard

financial abuse
fights over nothing
fight, flight, freeze or fawn
first voice
fixed condition
fleas
flashback
flying monkeys
fog
follow-up hoover
fuel reaction
fuel / fuel source
future faking

G _____ 94

gaslighting
glass with holes
golden child
golden period
good narc - bad narc
grandiose narcissist
grandstanding
grand finale
granting
grey rock
grooming
grooming phase

H _____ 100

harem
head living

healthy narcissism
heart living
honeymoon period
hurt to rescue
hyper emotions
hyper-vigilance

I ———————————————————— 104

initial grand hoover
idealization
idealization phase one
identify shift
identify theft
impending doom
individuation
inner critic
integrating behavior
intellectual empathy
intermittent reinforcement
intermittent explosive disorder
internal guidance system
invalidation
invert narcissist
invisible child
invisible self
irritable male syndrome
is factor
isolation

J ———————————————————— 110

jokasti syndrome

jekyll hyde syndrome

k _____ **111**

kool aid syndrome

L _____ **112**

learned helplessness
linen cupboard syndrome
lost child syndrome
love addiction
love bombing
low contact

M _____ **115**

madonna complex
magical thinking
malign return
malignant narcissist
marginalizing:
mascot
mask
mask slipping
mean and sweet cycle
megalomaniac

mental abuse

mental disorder

minimalizing

mirroring

moving the goal post

moving the start line

mr / ms breathy

mr / ms long face

mr / ms opposite

my way or the highway syndrome

mythical thinking

N _____ 123

narcissist

narcanese

narcissistic abuse cycle

narcissistic abuse syndrome

narcissistic brain damage

narcissistic branding

narcissistic bubble

narcissistic collapse

narcissistic conditioning

narcissistic consumption

narcissistic despair cycle

narcissistic environment

narcissistic envy

narcissistic family system

narcissistic fatigue

narcissistic filter

narcissistic induced depression

narcissistic induced fear

narcissistic injury

narcissistic mind reading

narcissistic mortification

narcissistic nit-picking

narcissistic perfectionism

narcissistic personality disorder (npd)

narcissistic projection

narcissistic rage

narcissistic spectrum

narcissistic storms

narcissistic supply

narcissistic tendencies

narcissistic victim syndrome

narcissistic view finder

narkie-ville

neglect

nice to nasty cycle

no contact

non-negotiables

non-productive arguments

non-validation

normalizing

O _____ **137**

object constancy

observe don't absorb system

out of integrity

overt narcissist

P _____ **139**

parasite

parental alienation syndrome

parentification

pathological critic

pathological lying

pawn

pedestal

personality disorder

physical abuse

playbook

pink cloud syndrome

pitch forking

plausible denial

poop in your soup

post abuse despair cycle

prediction and preparation

present time living

projection

predictive awareness

primary resource

private shaming

psychic virus

psychopath

public shaming

R _____ **148**

rage disorder

reactive anger

recharge

reciprocity

reality check

reality warping

redefining

resigned passiveness

resolution

respite

righteous anger

rumination

safe and sacred place

sadistic narcissist

sanctuary wounds

scapegoat

scorecard

segmented love

self-esteem

self-love

self-love deficiency disorder

self-love foundation

self-partnering

self-regulating

self-soothing

secondary resource

sexual harassment

secret shaming

self-care

self-rescue

shame dumping

shape shifting

should shaming

silent rule book

silent treatment

sld friends

smear campaign

somatic narcissist

sociopath

soul trauma

space pollution

space nazi

spectrum

sphere of influence

spiritual abuse

stonewalling

spousal abandonment syndrome

sun syndrome

survival mode

sustainable narcissism

syndrome

symptoms of narcissism

T _____ **167**

target

time circus

tertiary fuel source

 the switch

toxic shame

trauma bonds

triangulation

PART 1

When a person finds themself drowning in the clutches and chaos of a narcissistic relationship, there comes an epiphanic moment when they realize they are living in a world entirely of its own.

I call this world **"Narkie-ville"** (pg.: 117); and truly, Narkie-ville *is* a world all its own. Just ask anyone of its torture camp survivors. Without pause they'll confirm that Narkie-ville is not only a world of its own, but it is also governed by rules of its own, it has a judicial, prison, and punishment system of its own; and what I personally discovered along my recovery journey, Narkie-ville even has a language of its own. I call this special dialect, **Narcanese** (pg.: 106).

narcanese
\[nar·can·ese]\
noun

the official "language" of the narcissist that includes both spoken, unspoken and written word as well as behaviors and tactics, that the narcissist uses while in an episode, to try to dupe, gain control or fuel source off others.

I learned to understand and eventually speak Narcanese after a long and destructive season in Narkie-ville. And thank God I finally did learn, as it was only by uncovering this covert language that I gained the power and clarity to find my roadmap out of a land of chaos and pain where I had been a blind citizen for years.

I say "blind citizen" because like most victims of narcissistic trauma, I did not consciously choose to move into Narkie-ville. My migration to the dark side was more like a cult onboarding, where due to my existing wounds and weaknesses I was preyed upon and seduced by a narcissist into believing that the world I was joining (which I *thought* was a land of love) was actually a war zone of manipulation and **fuel sourcing** (pg.: 77.) One that after sucking the near life out of me, left me with **Complex Post-**

Traumatic Stress Disorder (pg.: 49), brain damaged **acute stress responses** (pg.: 24) not to mention years of therapy where I slowly and *effortfully* had to recover from **narcissistic abuse syndrome** (pg.:107), a unique diagnosis specific to narcissistic abuse trauma victims that happens because the quest for **fuel** (pg.:77) is camouflaged as the pursuit of "love", and where relationship breakdowns that normally have a dialogue for **resolution (**pg.:132), were met with **word salad** (pg.:161) and **stonewalling (**pg.:146), that leaves a person **gaslit (**pg.:79) and in a state of **f.o.g** (pg.:76).

If you don't understand what some of those words mean, don't feel bad. These words are the language of Narcanese, and in this book, **Narc.tion.ar.y,** I will teach you how to understand and speak this covert language so you too can find your way out of Narkie-ville and begin healing from the trauma of narcissistic abuse.

About this Book

Before we begin our lessons on Narcanese, I want to first introduce you to my mother. Her name is Alicia. For whatever reason, we have always called her

"Momsie", and she, like many mothers, is nothing short of amazing.

Momsie is a special soul. Born in El Salvador, this blonde-haired, hazel-eyed, 5'1" beauty came to the United States and married my Oklahoma dad Ken, when she was just 18. Together they had 4 kids.

As a foreigner in America, especially in the 1960's Momsie walked to the beat of a different drum. Which as a result, so did we kids. For instance, we were the children in church wearing boho funky styles and sporting bowl or shag haircuts long before "the bowl" or "the shag" existed. We ate yogurt, avocados, and pomegranates as afterschool snacks, before they were part of pop culture. And we were also the kids who while other children learned ballet or tap, Momsie was teaching us the Hula in our living room.

Momsie always was, and to this day at 82, still is, a colorful presence: A forever childlike spirit with the gift of great storytelling, and most notable, the ability to retain odd facts and information that somehow became a staple in her unconventional, yet always on

When however, what is plaguing you has a name, you are then in a position of power, as it becomes real. And when it is real, you can then grab ahold of it, and pull it into your life and fix, repair or restore it.

Or... if it is something that doesn't best serve you, you can push it out of your life, and never allow its toxicity to enter your life again."

Narc.tion.ar.y is built on this Momsieism, and the goal of this book is to teach narcissistic trauma survivors how to "give name" to the many ghosts that live within the world of narcissism, narcissistic abuse, narcissistic trauma, and narcissistic abuse recovery. *Or, as I am passionate about helping trauma victims recovery, the goal if narcissism is something that doesn't best serve you, this book will "give name" to the man ghosts so you can push it out of your life, and never allow its toxicity to enter your life again."*

Memo from Normal Land®:
"We have the right as adults,
to live ghost-free lives."

How to Use this Dictionary

This dictionary is a recovery tool designed to assist victims of narcissistic abuse on their road to recovery. The methodology of this book is threefold:

1. To give a name and a clear definition to the "ghosts (i.e. the strange and threatening behaviors of the narcissist) that live in Narkie-ville."

2. To give name and definition to the trauma that has been caused by living in Narkie-ville.

3. To give name and definition to the power words of recovery to overcome narcissistic trauma.

The definitions in this book have been formatted into what I call "narcissistic specific definitions." For example this means that though the word "abuse" is a general term that crosses many territories, the definition of *abuse* in Narc.tion.ar.y is a specific description as to how it applies to narcissism.

The words in Narc.tion.ar.y are grouped in one of three categories. These three categories are:

💣 **Abuse Techniques:** These words are the abuses, manipulations, and shenanigans of the narcissist. They are identified in this book by an emoji bomb.

☹ **Trauma Wounds:** These words are the aftereffects of narcissistic abuse trauma. They are identified in this book by an emoji sad face.

☼ **Recovery Words:** These words are the professional terminology, and the goal marks of healing and recovery. These words are identified in this book by an emoji sun.

About the Words

This dictionary has over 350 words linked to the world of narcissism, narcissistic abuse, narcissistic abuse trauma and narcissistic abuse recovery. There origins come from four different places.

1: Tracy Land Words:
Some of the words in this dictionary are my own "ghosts" that I gave name to.

For example, **Mr. / Ms. Breathy** (pg.:103). This ghost got its name because along my recovery journey every time my narcissist would address me as "Mr. Breathy", it meant that I caused a **narcissistic injury** (pg.:112). As a result, this meant a **fight-over-nothing** (pg.:74) or a punishment of some sort was about to ensue. The stress of this **impending doom** (pg.: 89) would send me into a **narcissistic despair cycle** (pg.: 189) where I would lose hours and sometimes days of my life in a state of trauma and survival.

However, by giving "Mr. Breathy" a name, meaning to give name to the non-verbal abuse technique, it empowered me to make space between me and the manipulation. That one step then allowed me to take pause and recognize that I was being *narcaneesed*, and rather than react to the ghost, I instead could then proactively hold onto my sanity and clarity while taking my healthy steps of recovery.

2: Professional Definitions:
Some of the words in this dictionary are professional terms as deemed by the DSM –5–TR (pg: 60) and other professional organizations. I have identified

these words by referencing the DSM within the definition, or identified the professional organization.

3: The Unknown:
As narcissism was officially identified 1898, some of the word origins are unknown, therefore no reference can be offered.

4: Influencer Culture:
Other words or terms in the book are the contributions of the amazing healers in the recovery industry. When I wrote this book it was not possible for me to remember where I learned each of these words or terms as when I began collecting my Narc.tion.ary, I was doing so only for myself. If however, you are one of these amazing heroes and you can claim "ghost rights" to any of the words in the Narc.tion.ary, please contact me so proper recognition can be given; and thank you for your contribution to narcissistic abuse recovery.

And Now We Begin

As we begin this journey, I would like to make note that this book is not intended to replace professional healing. This book is to serve solely as resource tool to assist you along your path of recovery and awareness.

That said, if while on your journey of recovery you discover any new ghosts, please reach out so that I can add it to this dictionary and share our healing contribution with the world.

There is much love here. Now, let's go slay some ghosts.

Dr. Tracy
@drtracykemble
@reclaimingmewithdrtracy

PART 2

The

Narc.tion.ar.y

A

abandoned child syndrome   category: ☹
\ [a·ban·doned ✦ child ✦ syn·drome] \

a proposed behavioral or psychological condition, caused by a parent abandoning a child either by physically leaving, failing to be emotionally present in their life, or by withholding affection, nurturing, or stimulation.

*"the victim of narcissistic abuse learned to normalize the abandonment because she/he suffered from **abandoned child syndrome** on account of her childhood trauma."*

abuse   category: 💣※
\ [abuse] \

the act, or acts, of the narcissist where he or she misuses words, money, religion, psychology, emotions, time, position, power, and/or the physical body to control, manipulate or harm another person for the benefit of the narcissist.

*"Narcissistic **abuse** comes in many forms including physical, sexual, emotional, psychological, spiritual, and financial."*

abuse amnesia
category:
\ [abuse • am·ne·sia] \

1) (Victim definition) also known as Dissociative Disorder, this condition is the inability of the victim to recall or remember the acts of abuse. This amnesia happens when the hippocampus (a region of the brain) shrinks after being exposed to long-term stress. It is the shrinkage of this part of the brain that causes the loss of memory.

2) (Narcissist Definition) a compulsive technique whereby the narcissist willfully believes or pretends to believe that traumatic events or circumstances he or she caused does not exist or did not happen, even when presented with evidence to the contrary.

*"due to the **abuse amnesia**, the victim was not able to clearly recall the verbal assaults. At the same time, after the abusive episode, the narcissist conveniently suffered from **abuse amnesia**, claiming no ownership or accountability for the abusive actions."*

abuse by proxy
category:
\ [abuse • by • prox·y] \

a form of abuse that occurs when a narcissist uses someone else or something else including friends, family, community, church, co-workers, court, or law enforcement to harm or control their victim.

The goal of abuse by proxy is to have other
people execute the acts of abuse for the
narcissist, with the aim of socially isolating,
manipulating, punishing, and discrediting the
victim. (See flying monkeys)
*"though the courts granted a restraining order, the victim
continued to experience **abuse by proxy** from the friends
and family of the narcissist."*

abuse cycle   category:
\ [a·buse • cy·cle] \
(See narcissistic abuse cycle)

abuse tactics   category:
\ [a·buse • tac·tics] \
the various techniques the narcissist uses against
the victim to control and manipulate them for fuel.
*"the narcissist used so many **abuse tactics** against the victim
that she/he lost the ability to hold onto her/his power."*

abusive expectations   category:
\ [a·bus·ive • ex·pec·ta·tions] \
unreasonable demands the narcissist places on the
victim. Examples include when the narcissist 1:
demands undivided attention or time from the
victim. 2: expects the victim to have only joy in

the abuser. 3: frequent demands for sex or being denied sex within the relationship. 4: when the victim is expected to put everything aside to satisfy the narcissist. 5: unrealistic lifestyle rules including keeping the house hospital clean or department store organized or prohibiting the victim from gaining weight or have any body issues that the abuser finds unacceptable.

*"the narcissist had physically **abusive expectations** of his victim by expecting her to be in swimsuit shape, in spite of just having a baby."*

abusive spending   category: 💣✳
\ [a·bus·ive • spend·ing] \

an abuse technique where one partner spends all the income without consulting or discussing the spending with the other.

*"the narcissist financially destroyed his/her partner because of their **abusive spending** habits that left the victim in deep credit card debt."*

acons   category: ✿
\ [a·cons] \

an acronym that stands for "adult children of narcissists."

*"if you are an **acon**, you run the risk of repeating the destructive cycle of narcissistic abuse, either as being a narcissist or by becoming the victim of narcissistic abuse.*

acute stress response   category: ☹
\ [a·cute ◆ stress ◆ re·sponse] \
(See Fight, Flight, Flee or Fawn)

adored to abhorred   category: 💣✳
\ [a·dored ◆ to ◆ ab·horred] \
(See bait and switch)

adult temper tantrum   category: 💣✳
\ [a·dult ◆ tem·per ◆ tan·trum] \
a meltdown, fit or emotional outburst by the narcissist when they do not get their way. Characterized by stubbornness, crying, screaming, violence, pouting, defiance, angry ranting, a resistance to attempts at pacification, and, in some cases, hitting and other physically violent behavior.
*"in the middle of the birthday dinner, the narcissist had an **adult temper tantrum** and made a scene that ruined the entire evening."*

aftershock
category: ☹

\ [a·fter·shock] \

similar to shock waves that continue to hit after an initial earthquake, aftershock is a condition or "shock" lodged in the body and emotions of the abuse victim. Aftershock presents itself after the narcissistic relationship is over and the victim can process the reality of the abuse they endured and survived. The condition can last one month to one year.

*"the victim was almost one year out of the relationship when his/her **aftershock** set in and he/she could finally understand what happened."*

altruistic narcissists
category: 💣✳

\ [al·tru·is·tic ♦ nar·cis·sists] \

a narcissist who excessively helps others and has a strong need to be needed and appreciated. While their intentions may seem pure, altruistic narcissists are not motivated by altruism. They they are motivated by a need for validation and appreciation. The goal of the altruistic narcissist is to use their helping behavior to control or take advantage of other people.

*"a classic **altruistic narcissist** is one who spends every Sunday volunteering at church, even if his family is home sick and needs his help."*

ambient abuse
category: 💣✳

\ [am·bient ✦ a·buse] \

a form of abuse that is stealth, subtle, and
underground where the ambient abuser creates
the false persona of altruism, benevolence, insight
and care towards the victim. The goal of ambient
abuse is to manipulate the victim into subscribing
to the difference of power, so the narcissist can
then control and abuse and the currents of
maltreatment without it being noticed, even by the
victims themselves.

*"the victim was traumatized because the **ambient abuse**
came from someone he thought cared for him."*

anticipated losses
category: ✿

\ [an·ti·ci·pa·ted ✦ loss·es] \

a recovery tool where the survivor gains the ability
to forecast the losses he or she will take when
leaving the narcissistic relationship.

*"she was able to make a sustainable exit plan because she
prepared for her **anticipated losses** in advance."*

anti-social personality disorder
category: 💣✳

\ [an·ti· ✦ so·cial ✦ per·son·al·ity ✦ or·der] \

a type of personality disorder on the narcissistic
spectrum in which an individual shows a strong

disregard for norms, morals and the law, or the rights and safety of others.   People with ASPD disorder show a willingness to manipulate and exploit others. They also have a lack of empathy and may engage in impulsive, irresponsible behavior to serve their own end needs.

*"People with **anti-social personality disorder** are dangerous individuals, not only because they can be aggressive and hostile, but also because they have little to no concern about what others think.*

api technique
category: ⚙

\[a·p·i ⬧ tech·nique] \

a recovery technique where the survivor will create an emotional space between themselves and the narcissist, which empowers them to no longer take things personal.

*"the victim used the **api technique** and kept his/her sanity by remembering that whatever the narcissist was saying, was just a reflection of him or herself."*

arguing in bad faith
category: 💣※

\[ar·gue·ing ⬧ in ⬧ bad ⬧ faith] \

an abusive arguing technique where the narcissist does not care about, nor tries to understand, the other person.   When arguing in bad faith the narcissist becomes dedicated to deliberately misunderstanding and mischaracterizing others, often to the point of absurdity. They will willingly be dishonest, deceptive and morally corrupt, while at the same time quickly accusing others of being dishonest, deceptive and morally corrupt.

"no matter what logic and reason was presented, the narcissist continued to **argue in bad faith** *just to keep the victim feeling crazy."*

assigning responsibility   category:
\[as·sign·ing • re·spon·si·bil·ity] \

an abuse technique where the narcissist controls their victim by telling him or her that they are responsible for the behavior and actions of the narcissist. Examples include statements such as, 1: "I did it because of you." 2: "I did it because of what happened." 3: "I said it because you made me mad." 4: "I said it because of what happened." 5: You made me want to ___ you." 6: "What's that ___ doing here?" 7: "How did this happen?"

"the victim ended-up apologizing for the argument and the abuse because the narcissist **assigned responsibility** *to her/him."*

assigning status   category:
\[as·sign·ing • sta·tus] \

a behavioral control technique where the

narcissist controls the victim by assigning status
in one of the five areas:
1) put downs: "You are the worst mother."
2) put ups: "You are the best diaper changer."
3) sentencing: "You are wrong / right to…"
4) categorizing: "All women are the same."
5) characterizing: "You are just like your mother."
*"a victim can get cornered into a no win situation when the
narcissist manipulatively **assigns status** to make them doubt
themself."*

awakening   category: ✿
\ [a·wake·n·ing] \

a recovery term that means, "to wake-up from a
sleep." In narcissistic abuse recovery, this term
is used to describe the season when the victim
begins to emerge from his or her fog and
recognizes the truths, traumas and abuses he or
she has survived.
*"Due to the chronic abuse, mind games and constant drama,
a victim does not have the mental energy or capacity to
recognize the daily chaos. When an awakening happens
though, the victim emerges from the narcissistic abuse coma
and reconnects with reality."*

B

baiting   category:

\ [bait·ing] \

the literal definition means, "to prepare a hook, trap, net, or fishing area with bait to entice fish or animals as prey." In narcissistic abuse, "baiting" is the technique the narcissist uses when he or she is trying to re-engage with the victim when "No Contact" is in place. Baiting is usually instigated with a friendly text or email with the goal of getting the victim to respond.

*"the narcissist was **baiting** his victim by sending friendly text to try to re-engage. Hopefully she/he will not respond."*

bait and switch   category:

\ [bait ⬧ and ⬧ switch] \

a technique where the narcissist first shows the victim "love and adoration" and then suddenly "switches" into loathing behavior. The goal of the bait and switch is to confuse the victim so the narcissist can gain control. This technique is also known as the "mean and sweet cycle", the "adore to abhor cycle" or the "nice and nasty cycle."

*"the victim was in a state of confusion because the narcissist did a **bait and switch** and changed all the dynamics in a moment."*

battles without resolution   category: ♠︎☀︎
\ [bat·tles ✦ with·out ✦ re·so·lu·tion] \

an abuse technique where the narcissist will create a no-win battle with the victim. The purpose of the *battle without resolution* is two-fold: 1: To crazy make their victim into confusion, exhaustion, and self-blame. 2: To create a fuel stream for the narcissist that he or she can draw upon for hours upon days as the victim is ruminating or trying to make amends for the breakdown of the relationship.

*"the narcissist creates a **battle without resolution** simply to extract on-going fuel from his or her victim."*

belief conflicts   category: ☹
\[be·lief ✦ con·flicts] \

when one or more of our beliefs causes us to live in conflict with how we behave.

*"the victim was stuck in the cycle of abuse because of his/her **belief conflicts** prohibited them from understanding how someone who claimed to love him/her (i.e., an ideology belief about love) treated him/her so poorly (i.e., a conflicting beahavior.)*

belief system   category:
\[be·lief ♦ sys·tem] \

in narcissism, it is a set of principles or tenets
selected only by the victim, that the victim
believes to be true and right for his or her life.
The belief system forms the basis of a victim's
decision–making skills.

*"only when the victim of narcissistic abuse changes their
belief system, will they heal from abuse."*

benign return   category:
\[be·nign ♦ re·turn] \

a term that describes a narcissistic technique of
fuel–sourcing where years after the relationship is
over, the narcissist will "return" either personally
or through flying monkeys with messages like "I
have always loved you."

*"after 5 years, the narcissist tried a **benign return** to see if
he/she could get fuel from his/her ex. Luckily it failed when
she/he did not respond."*

bidding   category:
\ [bidd·ing] \

when the narcissist organizes his or her flying
monkeys to lead a smear campaign about the
victim.

"the next step in the narcissist smear campaign was to

approach the co-workers of his/her victim and do some bidding."

big / bigger syndrome   category: 💣※
\ [big ✦ big·ger ✦ syn·drome] \

a narcissistic abuse technique where the victim
will implement a boundary to defend him or
herself against the narcissist (i.e., he or she gets
"big"), and the narcissist will then react by
"getting bigger" to regain control. Acts of bigger
can include yelling, towering, threats to leave, or
threats or acts of harm.

"the victim was too afraid to stand up to the narcissist
because anytime she/he held a boundary, the narcissist
*would respond with a **big/bigger** approach, which escalated*
the arguments to dangerous levels."

birthrights   category: ✿
\ [birth·rights] \

any right or privilege to which a person is entitled
by birth. In narcissistic recovery, birthrights, also
known as relationship rights, include the Right to
Joy, the Right to Safety, the Right to Individuality,
the Right to a First Voice, the Right to
Recognition, the Right to Evolve, the Right to
Clarity, the Right to Truth, the Right to Peace, the
Right to Separateness, and the Right to

Congruency and More. (See the Reclaiming Me
program for all survivor rights)
*"a narcissist is able to mistreat a victim because most have
never been explained their **birthrights**."*

black-and-white thinking

category:

\ [black ◆ and ◆ white think·ing] \

an irrational thinking characterized by the "all-or-
nothing" principle. People with this unrealistic
expectation do not see gray areas in most
situations; hence, they often feel frustrated, bitter,
and disappointed.

*"also known as polarized thinking, **black and white thinking**
does not allow the victim to express the many colors of the
Self."*

black cloud syndrome

category:

\ [black ◆ cloud ◆ syn·drome] \

 (narcissistic definition) a syndrome that stems
from the narcissist's belief that other people do
not have the right to feel happy without the
narcissist's consent. As a form of punishment, the
narcissist will cause drama or trauma to "darken
the spirits" of those who have happiness outside
of the narcissist.

 (victim definition) a syndrome that develops
when exposed to chronic narcissistic abuse where

the victim is trained not to shine bright or have happiness without permission of the narcissist. Over time, the victim will avoid situations where he or she is celebrated and suffer bouts of depression because subconsciously they believe their personal happiness causes punishment.

*"it was a disappointing evening because the victim of abuse could not celebrate her success because the narcissist **black clouded** her moment, by punishing her with the silent treatment.*

blame shifting   category: 💣※
\ [blame ✦ shift·ing] \

an abuse technique where the narcissist avoids responsibility of a wrongdoing, claiming that the abuse would not have occurred but for the previous actions of the victim.

*"clearly the narcissist was **blame shifting** when he turned the conversation from what the narcissist did wrong, to what the victim did wrong."*

body language abuse   category: 💣※
\ [body ✦ lang-u·age ✦ a·buse] \

a form of control where the narcissist uses body language, also known as nonverbals, to control their victim. Controlling gestures include sulking, refusing to talk, withdrawal of affection, strutting

and posturing, stomping out, walking away, hitting
something, kicking something, or driving recklessly.
*"the narcissist never had to hit the victim. He/she used
non-verbal **abusive body language** to send the message."*

boiling frog syndrome   category: ●✳☹
\ [boil·ing ✦ frog ✦ syn·drome] \

a syndrome where the narcissist will slowly bring
up "the heat" so the victim cannot see the abuse
and danger. The term comes from recovery
expert Melody Beattie, who states "If you put a
frog into a pot of boiling water, it will jump
straight out to save its life. However, if you put a
frog into cold water and slowly bring it to the boil,
the frog will remain unaware of the heat and
slowly cook itself to death."
*"the victim did not sense the danger because the narcissist
used the **boiling frog** method to slowly gain control."*

boundary   category: ✿
\ [bound·ry] \

the invisible healthy boarders each person sets
for oneself that marks the limits of one person
from another.
*"the narcissist cannot stand when a victim implements a
boundary.*

boundary push(es)   category: 💣☀

\ [bound·ry ✦ push·es] \

an abuse technique where the narcissist slowly chips away at the victim's desires, thoughts, fears, and beliefs until the narcissists receives full power of control over the victim.

*"the take over did not happen all at once. Instead, it happened by a series of small **boundary pushes** that were so slight, the victim did not see it happening until it was too late."*

boundary push-backs   category: ✿

\ [bound·ry ✦ push ✦ backs] \

a recovery technique the survivor uses towards the narcissist where they implement small steps of change (i.e., boundary push-backs) to retake their life.

*"the first steps the victim made to reclaim his/her life was to give small **boundary push-backs** to the narcissist's control."*

brainwashing   category: 💣☀

\ [brain·wash·ing] \

(See narcissistic conditioning)

branding   category: ☹
\[brand·ing] \

when the narcissist pressures, insists, coerces, or guilts the target into getting a permeant marking on their being as a sign of "love", ownership and or loyalty to the narcissist.

*"upon examination, the victim was notably **branded** with the name of the narcissist on the lower belly."*

broken heart syndrome   category: ☹
\ [brok·en ✦ heart ✦ syn·drome] \

a temporary heart condition that is brought on by stressful situations and extreme emotions. People with broken heart syndrome may have sudden chest pain or believe they are having a heart attack. In extreme cases, it can lead to death.

*"the victim came to the hospital with chest pain, but after examined and no heart distress was found, she was diagnosed with **broken heart syndrome**."*

broken record syndrome   category: ☹
\ [brok·en ✦ re·cord ✦ syn·drome] \

a stress response syndrome that causes the target of narcissistic abuse to repeat themselves. It arises when the victim of narcissistic abuse is stonewalled by a narcissist, and they feel unheard.

"When the victim's need to be heard is ignored by the

narcissist, the victim will start to repeat themselves and sound like a broken record. Many think this is a sign of weakness, but it is actually a cry for help."

bubble living
category: 🅑✳

\ [bub·ble ✦ liv·ing] \

(See narcissistic bubble)

burdening
category: 🅑✳

\ [bur·den·ing] \

an abuse technique where the narcissist puts all the financial burden on the victim by refusing to work, continuously finds excuses why they cannot work, or is not able to keep a job or income.

*"she/he didn't realize that much of the stress came from the narcissist **burdening** her/him with all the financial responsibility."*

burnout
category: ☹

\ [burn·out] \

a trauma wound and medical condition prompted by narcissistic fatigue. Burnout is a state of physical, mental, and emotional exhaustion brought on by excessive and prolonged stress.

*"after tolerating and absorbing the extreme stress from the narcissistic abuse, the victim ended-up in the hospital with symptoms of **burnout**."*

C

cerebral narcissist
category:

\ [ce·re·bral ✦ nar·ci·ssist] \

a narcissist who bases their entire narcissistic
tendency and self-image on their mind or
intellectual pursuits.

*"the professor is clearly a **cerebral narcissist** as he/she
thinks he/she is smarter than the rest of us."*

character assassination
category:

\ [char·ac·ter ✦ ass·ass·ig·na·tion] \

an abuse technique where the narcissist
assassinates the character of the victim.
Examples of character assassination include 1: an
exaggeration of mistakes. 2: gossiping about their
partner's past failures and mistakes. 3: lying to
friends, family, and coworkers about the abuse
victim, especially if the couple is estranged. 4:
humiliating, criticizing, or discounting the
achievements of the victim. 5: making fun of or
joking about the victim.

*"when the narcissist realized the victim was not coming
back, he/she began a **character assassination** campaign to
the friends and family to discredit the victim's reputation."*

chess syndrome   category: 💣※
\ [chess ✦ syn·drome] \

a narcissistic abuse technique where the
narcissist keeps their victim in a constant state of
"check", as in the game of Chess. This constant
state of "you are in danger" causes the victim of
abuse to suffer from chronic anxiety.

*"the victim suffered severe anxiety because of the on-going
threat she felt due to the chess syndrome abuse tactic."*

circular argument   category: 💣※
\ [cir·cu·lar ✦ ar·gu·ment] \

an abuse technique where the narcissist creates
backward arguments where their argument is on
feeling instead of fact, thereby not allowing the
victim to logically defend his or her position.

*"the circular argument had no resolution because the victim
could not argue based on fact."*

classic narcissist   category: 💣※
\ [class·ic ✦ nar·ci·cist] \

a person whose set of behaviors and
characteristics are identified by a pattern of
grandiosity, self-centered focus, need for
admiration, self-serving attitude, and a lack of
empathy or consideration for others.

*"due to his/her self-centered disposition, the therapist was able to diagnose him/her as a **classic narcissist***.

cluster b   category: 💣💥
\ clus·ter ◆ b] \

a series of personality disorders as defined in the DSM-IV and DSM-5-TR. They are characterized by impulsive, self-destructive, emotional behavior and sometimes incomprehensible interactions with others. They include antisocial personality disorder, borderline personality disorder, histrionic personality disorder and narcissistic personality disorder.

*"luckily, **cluster b** complex can be diagnosed by a professional therapist and with long term support and therapy, it is treatable."*

closure fog   category: ☹
\ [clo·sure ◆ fog] \

when the relationship with a narcissist suddenly ends, the victim is left with many questions. This state of confusion is called closure fog. Closure fog happens because narcissistic relationships ends with the Discard, where there is no dialogue, explanations or final good-byes, which are needed for closure. This abrupt exit leaves the victim flummoxed and in a state of confusion.

"when the narcissist left without warning, his/her victim slipped into closure fog."

co-dependency   category: ☹
\ [co·de·pen·den·cy] \

a psychological condition or relationship in which a person with low self-esteem or self-love deficiency disorder possesses a strong desire for others' approval or has an unhealthy attachment to a controlling or manipulative person. (See Self-Love Deficiency Disorder for more)

"every person in a narcissistic relationship suffers from co-dependency."

cognitive dissonance   category: ☹
\ [cog·ni·tive s dis·so·nance] \

a negative mental state of distress where the victim of narcissistic abuse has two conflicting thoughts about the same subject. Cognitive Dissonance happens when the harmony between one's belief system and actions are misaligned.

"cognitive dissonance happens when the victim of narcissistic abuse creates excuses to accept or justify the abuses and destructive behaviors of the narcissist."

cognitive empathy
category:

\ [cog·ni·tive ✦ em·pa·thy] \

an abuse technique where the narcissist uses
"fake" empathy to discover the weaknesses or
vulnerabilities of their target.

*"my narcissist never had empathy for me. He/she was using
cognitive empathy by telling me that they too experienced
many of the same traumas I had."*

compassion fatigue
category: ☹

\ [com·pan·ion ✦ fa·tigue] \

the negative side effect of over-giving.

*"the victim collapsed on account of compassion fatigue
because she continued to give her narcissist chances."*

communal narcissist
category: 💣

\ [co·mmun·al ✦ nar·ci·sist] \

a type of narcissism in which the narcissist
expects and needs attention and praise for their
generous acts. Also known as an altruistic
narcissist, he or she receives validation from the
community around them by doing good deeds or
acts of community service.

*"it was difficult at first to see that he/she was a communal
narcissist because on the surface he/she seemed so
altruistic."*

constant analysis   category: ☹

\ [con·stant ✦ anal·y·sis] \

(See rumination)

constant chaos   category: 💣※

\ [con·stant ✦ cha·os] \

an abusive fuel supply technique where the
narcissist creates continual upheavals of chaos.
The goal of constant chaos is to extract large
amounts of fuel from the victim and anyone else
involved in the chaos. Samples of constant chaos
include:

1: unnecessary arguments over nothing.

2: sudden illnesses, accidents and traumas that
happen if the attention or priority is shown to
other people rather than the narcissist.

3: deliberate arguments and conflicts to keep the
center of attention on the narcissist.

4: the inability to enjoy harmony and peace, and
as such creates constant disruptions.

5: negative moods that govern the environment of
the relationship.

*"there was never time for the victim to recover because of
the **constant chaos** the narcissist created."*

constant criticism   category:
\ [con·stant ✦ cri·ti·ci·sm] \

an abuse technique where the narcissist constantly finds faults in the victim and blames him or her for anything that goes wrong in the relationship.

"the victim suffered from extreme insecurity because the narcissist bombarded her/him with constant criticism."

contagious insanity   category: ☹
\ [con·ta·gious ✦ in·san·i·ty] \

the mental illnesses (i.e., a disruption in healthy mentality) the victim of narcissistic abuse develops on account of the narcissist's mental illness.

"the abuse victim suffered his own mental illness that was caused by contagious insanity."

controlling behaviors   category:
\ [con·troll·ing ✦ be·hav·i·ors] \

an abuse control technique where the narcissist deprives the victim of commonly held resources that are essential to his or her well-being and sense of integrity and sanity. Examples of controlling behavior include:

1: controlling time

2: grandstanding

3: controlling space

4: controlling finances

5: controlling body language

6: reality defining

7: motive defining

8: responsibility assigning

9: status assigning

*"a narcissist's **controlling behaviors** violates the human rights of the victim."*

core identity

category: ✿

\ [core ◆ i·den·ti·ty] \

the essence of who a person is.

*"narcissistic abuse is so dangerous because it chips away at the victim's **core identity**."*

couching

category: 💣☀

\ [couch·ing] \

an abuse technique where the narcissist will wrap an insult to look like a concern. For example, "I just don't want you to look like an idiot / loser in front of people."

*"the narcissist perfected the art of the insult when he started **couching** his victim with underhanded insults."*

covert narcissist   category: 💣※
\ [co·vert ✦ nar·cis·sist] \

a form of narcissism where narcissistic traits are
hidden. A covert narcissist comes across as highly
sensitive, introverted, anxious, depressed,
envious, defensive, hostile, moody or bitter,
and/or lacking self-esteem.

*"at first I thought she/he was so kind and sensitive. But
time would tell that she/he was actually a **covert narcissist**
as she/he controlled everyone through her moods and
defensiveness."*

covert love bombing by-proxy   category: 💣※
\ [co·vert ✦ love ✦ bomb·ing ✦ by ✦ prox·y] \

an abuse technique where the narcissist will use
flying monkeys to send "news" to the victim
about his or her break-up despair. The goal of
covert love bombing by-proxy is to love bomb
their victim via other people in hopes of 1:
getting the victim to feel sorry for the narcissist,
or 2: get the victim to believe the narcissist has
changed, and return to the relationship.

*"the narcissist used **covert love bombing by-proxy** by
having his sister call her and tell her that he was suffering
since their break-up.*

cptsd
category:☹

\ [c·p·t·s·d] \

known as complex post trauma stress disorder,
cptsd is a specific narcissistic abuse stress
related condition that in 2016, was recognized by
the World Health Organization as a condition that
results when a person is exposed to chronic on-
going traumatic events or situations. The victims
of narcissistic abuse, suffer from CPTSD, versus
PTSD. CPTSD stands for Complex Post-
Traumatic Stress Disorder, and it has 5 specific
symptoms: 1) Chronic Emotional Flashbacks of
the trauma. 2) Difficulty controlling one's
emotions & Dissociation. 3) Toxic Shame/
Codependence 4) Abandonment Disorder 5) A
Vicious Inner Critic and Social Anxiety Disorder.
*"unless the victim of abuse understands the difference
between PTSD versus CPTSD, they will not heal."*

crazymaking
category: 💣✳

\ [cra·zy • mak·ing] \

(See gaslighting)

crumbs
category: 💣✳

\ [crumbs] \

also known as "crumbing", this is an abuse

technique where the narcissist keeps the victim "working" for their love. It happens in stage 2 of the narcissistic cycle of abuse when suddenly the narcissist will cut back on the "love" they used to give the victim, all with the goal of keeping the victim hooked as a constant stream of supply or fuel.

"it was obvious that phase two of the abuse cycle kicked-in as the victim responded with desperation to the narcissist's crumbs of love."

cycle of abuse

category: 💣※

\ [cy·cle ◆ of ◆ a·buse] \

(See narcissistic abuse cycle)

D

dark tetrad
category: 💣✳

\ [dark ♦ tet·rad] \

the four personality traits that are correlated with criminal and antisocial behavior which include: narcissism, psychopathy, Machiavellianism, and sadism. Although social research demonstrates that each of the four has distinct qualities, they also have some overlapping characteristics, including a lack of empathy and remorselessness and a willingness to exploit and manipulate.

"dark tetrad can only be diagnosed by a professional therapist after they meet the client personally."

deal breaker
category: ⚙

\ [deal ♦ break·er] \

a set of standards and boundaries the victim of narcissist abuse learns to set for him or herself that if violated will end the relationship. Deal breakers are anything the person in recovery sets for his or herself to make life safe.

"the victim of abuse finally had a clear vision on what her/his deal breakers were. That is when she/he was able to set boundaries and mean it."

defining motive

category:

\ [de·fin·ing ✦ mo·tive] \

a control technique where the narcissist will tell the victim *why* he or she has done what they have done, as though the narcissist knows their internal motives.

*"when a narcissist tries to **define the motive** of their victim, it is nothing more than the narcissist's attempt of control."*

defining reality

category:

\ [de·fin·ing ✦ re·al·ity] \

a form of narcissistic abuse where the narcissist defines the reality of their victim by denying certain events happened, by discounting the victim's feelings, or by accusing the victim of trying to start a fight.

*"a form of crazymaking is when the narcissist tries to **define the reality** of the victim. Healing however is when the victim realizes that his or her truth, regardless of validation, is the only truth that matters."*

defining truth

category:

\ [de·fin·ing ✦ truth] \

a control technique where the narcissist will attempt to define the truth of the victim by using statements such as, "you don't know what you're talking about." Or, "That is not how you feel."

*"when a narcissist tries to **define the truth** of their victim, it is nothing more than the narcissist's attempt of control. Healing is to remember that your truth is your truth."*

deflecting
category:

\ [de·flect·ing] \

an abuse technique within arguments where the narcissist will shift attention from what he or she has done wrong, to what the victim has "done wrong."

*"the purpose of **deflection** is for the narcissist to avoid any responsibility for their toxic behavior or address any needs of the victim."*

delusional narcissist
category:

\ [de·lu·sion·al ✦ nar·ci·ssist] \

a narcissist who is very grandiose in their beliefs and are often full of stories that are so over-the-top that they lack belief.

*"the only good thing about **delusional narcissism** is that their extreme behavior is easy to spot."*

de-masking
category:

\ [de·mask·ing] \

(see unmasking)

denial
category: ☹

\ [de·ni·al] \

an emotional state of the grieving cycle that the victim of abuse slips into when they are unable to process the severity of the situation.

*"some think that **denial** is stupidity. But in truth it is a form of survival."*

detectiving
category: ☹

\ [de·tec·tiv·ing] \

a trauma survival technique where the victim incessantly googles, researches or tries to find answers to the world of narcissism. Questions include "Is this normal?" "What is wrong with me / him / her." Am I crazy?" Or any other search that will help the victim to understand the fog.

*"every victim of narcissistic abuse uses **detectiving** when they begin to feel that something is wrong."*

devaluation phase
category: 💣

\ [de·val·u·a·tion • phase] \

phase two in the narcissistic abuse cycle where the narcissist switches from love and praise of their target to putdowns and punishments. During this phase, the narcissist is monitoring the trauma responses of the victim looking for reactions such as crying, depression, chasing, confusion, shame, sulking, etc. These responses are important to the narcissist because they provide fuel / supply.

*"it is important to know that once the **Devaluation Phase** has started, the relationship will never go back to the good days.*

diminished identity   category: ☹
\ [di·min·ished • iden·ti·ty] \

an aftermath of narcissistic abuse where the victim loses their clarity and lack of core identity. The emotional loss and dramatic change of oneself is a result of the slow and systematic erasing of their soul, perpetrated by the ongoing abuses of the narcissist.

*"healing from **diminished identity** and reinstating one's core identity is one of the most important processes in the recovery journey."*

director of judgement   category: 💣✳
\ [di·rec·tor • of • judge·ment] \

a self-appointed position the narcissist chooses for him or herself where they believe they have the right to cast all and final judgement on people and situations without input from anyone else.

*"as the self-appointed **director of judgement**, the narcissist believed he/she had the right to assign value to the entire group."*

discard
category: 💣✳

\ [dis·card]\

phase 3 in the narcissistic cycle of abuse where the narcissist will "throw away" the victim and leave the relationship suddenly or without notice, often moving onto another relationship.

*"victims describe the **discard** as 'being put out like trash."*

dissociation
category: 🙁

\ [dis·so·ci·a·tion] \

a mental condition caused by continued stress or trauma. Dissociation encompasses the feeling of daydreaming or being intensely focused, as well as the distressing experience of being disconnected from reality.

*"**dissociation** can be terrifying for those who experience it. Treatment is available through a trained professional."*

dissociative amnesia
category: 🙁

\ [dis·so·-cia·tive ✦ am·ne·sia] \

(See abuse amnesia)

distancing
category: 💣✳

\ [dis·tanc·ing] \

an abuse technique where to punish the victim, the narcissist will withdrawal attention or affection until he or she gets what they want.

*"**distancing** is often combined with the silent treatment to form the ultimate form of punishment on the victim."*

divide and conquer
category:

\ [di·vide ✦ and ✦ con·quer] \

an abuse technique where the narcissist gains control of their victim by separating them from people.

*"the goal of the **divide and conquer** technique is to create division, as once they can isolate the target, the narcissist can manipulate and dominate him or her."*

dog whistling
category:

\ [dog ✦ whis·tling] \

an abuse technique similar to baiting, except it is where the narcissist will publicly or privately antagonize the victim into a response so they can extract fuel.

*"the narcissist approached his ex in public and started **dog whistling** at her new boyfriend hoping for a fight."*

domestic violence
category:

\ [do·mes·tic ✦ vi·o·lence] \

as defined by the United States Department of Justice, Domestic Violence is "a pattern of abusive behaviors in any relationship that is used by one partner to gain or maintain power and control over another intimate partner."

*"**domestic violence** affects 1 in 4 women in the United States and 1 in 3 women globally according to the United Nations. One in 11 men experience domestic violence."*

domination   category: 💣※
\ [do·min·a·tion] \

a control technique where the narcissist uses threats of abandonment, rejection, harm or loss whenever the victim makes choices not "approved" by the narcissist.

*"**domination** is a powerful abuse technique, especially for victims with abandonment trauma."*

do-over   category: ☼
\ [do • o·ver] \

a recovery tool for the victim where when after he or she realizes they responded in a less than powerful manner, they return to the person they encountered and take a "do-over" as a healthy response.

*"the victim was able to retrain herself by taking a **do-over** to state her authentic needs."*

dosing
category:
\ [dos·ing] \

an abuse technique where after a cruel phase of abuse, the narcissist will provide a morsel of positive attention.

*"the narcissist uses **dosing** as a way to re-addict their target."*

double binding
category:
\ [dou·ble_♦ bind·ing] \

an abuse technique where the narcissist puts the victim in a "damned if you do and damned if you don't" paradox. A classic sign of double binding is when after a fallout or argument, the victim presents options or avenues of reconnection or repair, yet all attempts are met with a negative response. Double binding can lead to Learned Helplessness.

*"the goal of **double binding** is to keep the victim in a state of confusion so the narcissist can extract fuel / supply."*

double standards
category:
\ [dou·ble ♦ stan·dards] \

the two sets of rules the narcissist sets for the relationship that includes one beneficial set of rules for the narcissist and one less-than or dehumanizing set of rules for everyone else.

*"a relationship based in authentic love does not have **double**

standards. It has only one standard that benefits both partners."

drama triangle   category: 💣✳
\[dra·ma • tri·an·gle] \

drama triangles are abusive environments the narcissist creates where the victim, the narcissist and a 3rd person are involved. This threesome involves "roles" that include the persecutor, the victim, and the rescuer, that when "played", keeps the drama alive.

"healing requires the victim to make the conscious choice to not participate in drama triangles."

drilling for fuel   category: 💣✳
\ [dra·ma • tri·an·gle] \
(See pitchforking)

dsm   category: ✿
\ [d·s·m] \

the standard classification of mental disorders used by mental health professionals in the United States. The full name is called the Diagnostic and Statistical Manual of Mental Health, currently in its 5th edition (DSM–5–TR.)

"narcissistic personality disorder (NPD) is one of many diagnosable conditions for those who are narcissists.

*Mentioned in the **Diagnostic and Statistical Manual** on Mental Disorders, edition five (DSM-5). The DSM-5 classifies NPD as a personality disorder and is an accurate diagnosis. Up to 6.2% of the general population have narcissistic personality disorder."*

E

ego-syntonic
category: 💣※

\ [ego ·syn·ton·ic] \

a personality disorder characteristic where the narcissist does not see their actions or attitudes as problematic.

"a sign of a narcissist is that they are ego-syntonics, therefore they don't see how their actions affect those around them."

emotional abuse
category: 💣※

\ [emo·tion·al ◆ a·buse] \

acts of verbal aggression or non-physical hostility that result in the loss of the victim's self-esteem or ability to trust one's own mental thought processes.

"the emotional abuse the narcissist projected onto the victim caused more trauma than a physical assault."

emotional bandwidth
category: ⚙

\ [emotion·al ◆ band·width] \

(See emotional threshold)

emotional blackmail
category: 💣☀

\ [emo·tion·al ✦ black ·mail] \

a control technique the narcissist uses where he or she threatens the victim with harm, pain, or loss if the victim does not comply with the narcissist's request(s) or demand(s). It is similar to hostage keeping, but rather than the victim being kept physically hostage, they are instead held emotionally hostage by the threats of harm or loss.

"a lot of victims experience **emotional blackmail** *when a narcissist threatens to share private information about them."*

emotional boundaries
category: ✿

\ [emo·tion·al ✦ bound·ar·ies] \

the boundaries and limits a survivor of abuse sets for him or herself when the narcissist attempts to distort their truth or fear them into submission.

"when a survivor of abuse starts implementing **emotional boundaries**, *the narcissist is no longer able to define their truth."*

emotional dissonance
category: ☹

\ [emo·tion·al ✦ dis·son·nance] \

a feeling experienced when one is forced to fake an emotion.

"many victims of abuse experience **emotional dissonance**

when they are forced to put on a happy face when what they really feel is excruciating emotional pain."

emotional face blindness   category: ●☀
\ [emo·tion·al • face • blind·ness]\

a gaslighting technique the narcissist uses when he or she pretends they do not notice the despair on their victim's face.

*"even though she was crying, the narcissist maintained **emotional face blindness**, showing no sympathy or empathy to her pain."*

emotional flashback   category: ☹
\ [emo·tion·al • flash·back] \

a stress response when the victim is triggered by something that reminds them of an abusive episode and instantly re-experiences the emotional trauma they were in during the abuse. (See trauma flashbacks)

*"when she/he walked by the perfume counter and smelled the scent of the ex-narcissist, she/he had an **emotional flashback** to the trauma filled Christmas."*

emotional home base   category: ✿
\ [emo·tion·al • home • base] \

a recovery term used to describe a person's inner truth and authentic first voice.

*"part of recovery is to reconnect to your **emotional homebase** and discover what your first voice says about things."*

emotional homelessness   category: ☹
\ [emo·tion·al ✦ home·less·ness] \

a term used to describe the loss of our sense of knowing where we belong and what our purpose is.

*"**emotional homelessness** is a feeling of wanting to go home, but you don't know where your emotional home base is anymore."*

emotional infection   category:
\ [emo·tion·al ✦ in·fec·tion] \

the power to infect beings with tainted and negative emotions.

*"the narcissist was so committed to destroying his ex's reputation that he/she **emotionally infected** the victim's co-workers with gossip and lies."*

emotional manipulation   category:
\ [emo·tion·al ✦ man·ip·u ·la·tion] \

the act of manipulating another person into an intense desired emotional state (such as love, passion or anger) to take advantage of them.

"after the target was identified, the narcissist began

emotionally manipulating her/him with gifts and trips so she/he believed the narcissist really cared."

emotional neglect   category:
\ [emo·tion·al • ne·glect] \

a distinct lack of action or support by one person in a relationship towards the other.

*"hallmarks of **emotional neglect** in a marriage is when there is a lack of emotional support resulting in partner's needs not being met."*

emotional neutral   category: ✿
\ [emo·tion·al • neu·tral] \

the act of not reacting or engaging with the narcissist when they are drilling for fuel.

*"when the survivor of abuse learns to become **emotionally neutral** with the narcissist, the narcissist will stop antagonizing them because he or she realizes they won't get fuel."*

emotional terrorist   category:
\ [emo·tion·al • terr·or·ist] \

a person who has an agenda to destroy the well-being of others by using emotionally loaded information, behaviors, innuendoes, direct assaults, inferences, rumors, and language, with no regard to the emotional well-being of the victim, but always to the benefit of the narcissist.

"the narcissist became an emotional terrorist by posting the private photos of her online."

emotional terrorism   category: 💣☀

\ [emo·tion·al ◆ terr·or·ism] \

(See emotional terrorist)

emotional thinking   category: ☹

\ [emo·tion·al ◆ think·ing] \

the unnecessary influence of emotions on the thought process that can lead to selective or imbalanced decisions.

"too much emotional thinking prompts a person to make irrational decisions because emotional thinking is void of logic."

emotional threshold   category: ☹

\ [emo·tion·al ◆ thresh·hold] \

the breaking point a victim reaches when experiencing narcissistic abuse.

"when the victim of narcissistic abuse has a nervous breakdown it means they have reached their emotional threshold and cannot handle the abuse any longer."

emotional vampire   category: 💣☀

\ [emo·tion·al ◆ vam·pire] \

a toxic person who drains another person of their

energy and leaves them feeling emotionally
exhausted.

*"**emotional vampires** have a parasitic quality in that they
provoke emotional reactions in others and "feed off" their
emotions as well as resources."*

empath   category: ✿
\ [em·path] \

a person who has the capacity to understand or
feel what another person is experiencing from
within their frame of reference. The capacity to
place oneself in another's position. Types of
empathy include cognitive empathy, emotional
empathy, somatic empathy, and spiritual empathy.

*"the reason that narcissists are attracted to **empaths** is that
the narcissist sees the feelings and emotions of the empath,
which is something the narcissist longs for."*

empathy deficient   category:
\ [em·path·y • de·fi·cient] \

a person who lacks the ability to understand or
feel what another person is experiencing from
within their frame of reference. The inability or
desire to place oneself in another's position.

*"all narcissist are **empathy deficient** because they cannot
put themselves in the shoes of another person."*

empty husk

category: 💣※

\ [emp·ty ✦ husk] \

a term used to describe how the narcissist feels
when their fuel tank is on empty.

*"when the narcissist is low on fuel, they feel like an **empty
husk** – something with no substance on the inside."*

enabler

category: ☹

\ [en·ab·ler] \

a partner, spouse or relative of the narcissist who
"normalizes" and even perpetuates the
narcissist's grandiose persona, extreme sense of
entitlement, and haughty attitude and behavior
toward others by absorbing the abuse and acting
as an apologist for it.

*"**enablers** have the delusion that they are the only ones who
can truly understand the narcissist and oftentimes sacrifice
or scapegoat their children to placate the narcissist."*

engaging

category: ☹

\ [en·gag·ing] \

the act of verbally responding or reacting to the
narcissist's overt and covert abuse tactics and
providing them fuel.

*"part of healing is realizing that by **engaging** with the
narcissist, we become a dose of fuel for them."*

enmeshment   category: ☹

\ [en·mesh·ment] \

a pattern in which there are no psychological boundaries between the family members, or between the victim and the narcissist.

"the two of them were so psychologically fused that their **enmeshment** *made them appear to have no separate identities."*

episodic   category:

\ [ep·i·so·dic] \

a term used to describe the active state of narcissism when the narcissist goes from benign behavior to ongoing abusive behavior.

"the victim was exhausted because the narcissist had been **episodic** *for days."*

erased syndrome   category: ☹

\ [e·raced ◆ syn·drome] \

(See diminished identity)

explosive disorder   category:

\ [ex·plo·sive ◆ dis·or·der] \

(See intermittent explosive disorder)

ex-recycling   category: 💣☀

\ [ex • re·cy·cling] \

when the narcissist stalks or tries to return to
their former partner / primary fuel source for
attention and control.

*"after the narcissist left the relationship for another person,
the narcissist then **ex-recycled** when that relationship went
bad and tried to win back their ex."*

F

fake empathy   category:

\ [fake ◆ em·pa·thy] \

   (See cognitive empathy)

false flattery   category:

\ [false ◆ flat·te·rey] \

   a form of love-bombing where the narcissist
   compliments the target in the area he or she
   may be insecure. The goal is twofold: 1) to
   get make the target to believe that the
   narcissist thinks they are special and 2) to get
   the target to fuel source the narcissist by
   getting a compliment in return.

   *"the narcissist was only offering up **false flattery** as a way
   to score points."*

false self   category:

\ [false ◆ self] \

   a pretend persona the narcissist presents to the
   world due to early childhood trauma. The False
   Self or Fictional Character is a cover for the
   shriveled-up True Self that lives within the
   narcissist.

"narcissists are so defensive because they live behind a false self and their biggest fear is being discovered for who they really are."

fauxpology   category: 💣✴

\ [faux·pol·o·gy] \

the false apology the narcissist gives their victim that lacks authenticity or accountability. This false apology is called a fauxpology because it is a fake apology. Examples of fauxpologies include: 1: "I'm sorry you think I'm such a disappointment."2: "I'm sorry you interpreted something so innocent as unfair."3: "I'm sorry you are so sensitive." 4: "I'm sorry you can't understand how others feel." 5: "I'm sorry you are so angry." 6: "I am sorry you feel that way."

"every time the victim received an apology it never felt authentic. That is because it was a fauxpology."

fear bombing   category: 💣✴

\ [fear ◆ bomb·ing] \

an abuse technique where the narcissist will 'bomb' their victim with unreasonable fear.

"fear-bombing is one of the ways the narcissist controls their victim. They paralyze them with fear."

fearland   category: ☹

\ [fear·land ✦ cit··ti zen·ship] \

a negative state of mind the victim of narcissistic abuse experiences where they are consumed with the negative repercussions of the narcissist.

*"the victim mentally lived in **fearland**, constantly ruminating over what the next move of the narcissist would be."*

fictional character   category: 💣※

\ [fict·tion·al ✦ char·ac·ture] \

the fantasy persona of either self or another person the narcissist creates where they either to justify their actions.

*"the narcissist was so angry that their target left that he/she created a **fictional character** of their victim and told exaggerated stories to ruin his/her reputation. Luckily no one believed the narcissist."*

final discard   category: 💣※

\ [final ✦ dis·card] \

stage 3 in the narcissistic abuse cycle, where the narcissist will suddenly "discard" their victim. The discard happens once the narcissist realizes they have squeezed every ounce of fuel out of their victim and have grown bored of the relationship.

*"on the **final discard**, the narcissist pushed the victim out of his life like trash."*

financial abuse   category: 💣✳

\ [fi·nan·tial ✦ a·buse] \

a form of financial abuse and control that is
identified by three characteristics: Withholding,
abusive spending and burdening.

*"the narcissist was **financially abusive** as she/he refused to
work a day of their life, expecting the victim to assume all
the bills."*

fights over nothing   category: 💣✳

\ [fights ✦ o·ver ✦ no·thing] \

an abuse technique the narcissist uses when a) he
or she is trying to avoid accountability. Or b) the
narcissist needs "reaction" for fuel.

*"the victim was so confused because of the chronic **fights
over nothing** that came out of nowhere and were based on
stuff that didn't make sense.*

fight, flight, freeze or fawn   category: ✿

\ [fight ✦ fight ✦ freeze ✦ fawn] \

the four ways people respond to threat.

fight: an aggressive response to perceived threat.

flight: running away from the danger.

freeze: unable to move or act against a threat.

fawn: doing whatever it takes to defuse a threat
including appeasing and going-along to get-along.

*"part of recovery is becoming aware of how you react when threatened. Do you **fight, flight, freeze or fawn?**"*

first voice   category: ✿
\ [first ✦ voice] \

the inner authentic thoughts, feelings, and beliefs a person has when no influenced by the narcissist or others.
*"we all have a **first voice**. It is our job it to find it, as when we do, no one can talk us out of our opinion."*

fixed condition   category: ☹
\[fixed ✦ con.di.tion] \

the inability to heal from the trauma.
*"the victim's **fixed position** completely blocked her/him from healing."*

fleas   category:
\ [fleas] \

a term used to describe how the bad habits of others can rub off on you if you remain in that person's presence. It comes from the saying "Lying down with dogs will give you fleas."
*"after years of being with a narcissist, I had narcissistic **fleas** as I was acting just as bad as the narcissist was."*

flashback
category: ☹

[flash·back] \

an involuntary recurrent memory in which a victim has a sudden, usually powerful, re-experiences of a past experience.

*"the sound of the Christmas music sent me into a spin because I had a **flashback** of when he/she ruined the entire holiday dinner."*

flying monkeys
category: 💣☀

\ [fly·ing   •   monk·eys] \

in modern psychology, a flying monkey is the person, or any group of people, who the narcissist enlists as allies, to do the bidding, or to inflict more torture on the victim.   The term comes from the movie *The Wizard of Oz* where the wicked witch enlisted "flying monkeys" to do her spying and dirty work.

*"the narcissist got reports on his ex by connecting with her/his co-workers, and like true **flying monkeys,** they kept spying on her/his, every move."*

fog
category: ☹

\ [fog] \

a term developed by Dana Morningstar that describes the traumatized state-of-mind of a

victim. Fog stands for fear, obligation and guilt.
*"she/he was in a total narcissistic **fog**, for years."*

follow-up hoover   category: 💣※
\ [fol·low ♦ up ♦ hoo·ver] \

a hoovering technique that takes place in the
latter part of the post–relationship phase where
the narcissist will try to contact the victim for
fuel. It can happen irrespective of whether the
victim was discarded or escaped.
*"five years after the break–up, the narcissist used **follow–up hoovering** to try to get a response out of me."*

fuel reaction   category: 💣※
\ [fuel ♦ re·ac·tion] \

the reaction of pain, elation or insanity that the
victim provides when the narcissist is *digging for fuel*.
*"after the narcissist abandoned her again, the victim fell into a deep depression. Yet by doing so, the narcissist received the **fuel reaction** the narcissist was searching for."*

fuel / fuel source   category: 💣※
\ [fuel ♦ source] \

(See narcissistic supply)

future faking   category: 💣※

\ [fu·ture ✦ fak·ing] \

an abuse conditioning technique where the
narcissist talks about the false future plans he or
she will have with the target.

*"the narcissist used **future faking** as a way to get the target
to fall in love."*

G

gaslighting   category: 💣※
\ [gas·light·ing] \

> also known as crazy making, this is an abuse
> technique where the narcissist will deny or lie
> about an event or chain of events. The goal of
> gaslighting is to cause confusion to the victim and
> make them self-doubt and "doubt of reality" so
> they can a: extract fuel, b: overtake the victim's
> possessions, have c: the victim deemed an unfit
> parent, and d: get away with their "other" life.
> *"because of all the **gaslighting**, the victim had no idea what
> was true and what was not."*

glass with holes   category: 💣※
\ [glass ✦ with ✦ holes] \

> a term used to describe the narcissist's never-
> satiable need for attention.
> *"feeding the narcissist's need for attention is like putting
> water in a **glass with holes**. It will simply never be
> enough."*

golden child

category: 💣✳ ☹

\ [gold·en ✦ child] \

> a term used to describe the narcissist's favorite
> child. The golden child is idealized as perfect
> and special compared to the other children.
>
> *"the narcissist perceives the **golden child** as a reflection*
> *of their own positive qualities and therefore will brag and*
> *boast about this child to receive fuel for him or herself.*
> *The golden child will often grow-up to be a narcissist.*

golden period

category: 💣✳ ☹

\ [gold·en ✦ per·i·od] \

> phase one in the narcissistic abuse cycle where
> the narcissist grooms the victim to "fall in love
> with them" by showering them in feel-good
> future faking fantasies, sexual ecstasies and
> false promises. It is the fact finding stage of
> the relationship where the narcissist tries to
> build trust with the victim so he or she will "let
> the narcissist in". The goal is for the narcissist
> to discover the victim's weaknesses, which will
> later be used as fuel sources.
>
> *"one thing that keeps a victim stuck in the cycle of abuse*
> *is that he or she tries to recapture the initial **golden***
> ***period** when things were good.*

95

good narc - bad narc

category:

\ [good·narc ✦ bad·narc] \

an abuse technique to extract information out of a victim, where they switch from nice to mean to nice to mean.

*"the narcissist went from **good narc to bad narc** when he/she realized he/she was not going to get the information he/she was fishing for."*

grandiose narcissist

category:

\ [gran·di·ous ✦ nar·ci·ssist] \

a form of narcissism where, unlike other narcissists who may have an underlying sense of insecurity or fragility, a person with grandiose narcissism believes, without doubt, that they *are* special, unique, and superior.

*"**grandiose narcissists** are more assertive and extroverted than their counterparts with standard NPD and will display such symptoms as very high confidence and self-esteem, superiority and entitlement, impulsivity, anger, hostility, and verbal or physical aggression when confronted, and exploitation of others."*

grandstanding
category:
\ [grand·stand·ing] \

a control technique used by the narcissist where
he or she monopolizes conversations by not giving
the victim their fair opportunity to speak; by
talking over their victim; or by answering
questions for the victim. Grandstanding can occur
both in public and private environments.

*"the goal of **grandstanding** is to silence the victim from
having a voice."*

grand finale
category:
\ [grand ◆ fi·nal·e] \

the term used to describe an over-the-top ending
of a relationship filled with drama, chaos, lies and
overall outrageousness.

*"the narcissist created one last **grand finale** before
discarding his/her victim."*

granting
category:
\ [grant·ing] \

a narcissistic form of abuse where the narcissist
believes a person can have good feelings only
with them, or only with whom or what they
approve of.

*"the narcissist only let the victim attend and enjoy
her/herself because he **granted** her permission."*

grey rock   category: ✿
\ [grey ◆ rock] \

a victim's survival tool where he or she responds
to the tactics of a narcissist with the personality
of a "grey rock", i.e. being <u>boring</u>, unemotional,
and neutral.

*"when I learned the skill of **grey rocking**, it stopped so many
fuel sourcing episodes."*

grooming   category: 💣✳
\ [groom·ing] \

the abusive process / technique where the narcissist
slowly mixes negative behavior and positive
behavior into the relationship with the goal of
wearing down a partner's boundaries so he or she
will accept abusive treatment. (See narcissistic
conditioning for more)

*"the narcissist spends months into years **grooming** their victim
into becoming the primary fuel source of the narcissist."*

grooming phase   category: 💣✳
\ [groom·ing ◆ phase] \

normally found in phase one of the narcissistic
cycle of abuse, the grooming phase is when the
narcissist is "grooming" their victim into addictive
love.

*"the purpose of the **grooming phase** is to get the victim "addicted" to the narcissist and therefore remain a constant fuel source even when the relationship shifts.*

H

harem

category:

\ [har·em] \

the admirers who offer supply for the
narcissist. These fuel sources consist of current
love interests, past love interests, people the
narcissist flirts with, family members, friends, co-
workers, or anyone that the narcissist keeps in his
or her circle who provides the narcissist with
positive fuel.

*"the narcissist was able to stay "filled" because he had an
entire **harem** fuel sourcing him."*

head living

category: ☹

\ [head ♦ liv·ing] \

a narcissistic trait and victim response where a
person thinks, reacts and creates choice in their
"head" (i.e., their mind).

*"**head living** will eventually burn out an empath."*

healthy narcissism   category: ✿
\ [health·y ✦ nar·ci·siss·m] \

a marker on the narcissistic spectrum that
identifies healthy and balanced levels of
narcissism.
*"we all need levels of **healthy narcissism** to keep the good
in and the bad out."*

heart living   category: ✿
\ [heart ✦ liv·ing] \

a recovery trait where the empath learns to
reconnect to her inner first voice and "gut",
before reacting.
*"when the victim remained in **heart living**, she was able to
realign with Divine intuition and make the right choices for
herself."*

honeymoon period   category:
\ [hon·ey·moon ✦ period] \

a term used in the classic cycle of abuse when
after an abusive incident, the couple slips into
denial, as though the abuse never happened, and
all is well.
*"after the explosion phase of abuse, the couple slipped back
into the **honeymoon period**, both hoping the incident will just
disappear."*

hurt to rescue
category:

\ [hurt ✦ to ✦ res·cue] \

an abuse technique cycle where the narcissist
will commit to helping the victim and then
intentionally withdrawal their help when it will
cause the most trauma to the victim.

*"the day healing began is when he/she refused to take the
narcissist's 'helpful hand' and finally stopped the* **hurt to
rescue** *cycle."*

hyper emotions
category:

\ [hy·per ✦ e·mo·tions] \

when a person's emotions are in an extreme state
and do not match the moment, they are facing.

"she was in a state of **hyper emotions** *and was not able to
assess the situation properly."*

hyper-vigilance
category: 💣※

\ [hyper·vig·i·lance] \

a victim's coping mechanism where he or she is in
an extreme state of alertness or caution due to an
on-going threat or attack. Hyper-vigilance is
emotionally and physiologically debilitating
because it drains the body's natural defense
system by constantly overloading it.

*"**hyper-vigilance** often leads to Complex Post-Traumatic Stress Disorder (CPTSD) and illness."*

I

initial grand hoover   category: 💣✳

\ [i·ni·tial ◆ grand ◆ hoo·ver] \

the "initial" bombardment that takes place *post* discard or post escape.

*"the goal of the **initial grand hoover** is to reconnect with the victim and attempt to bring him or her back into the cycle of abuse."*

idealization   category: 💣✳   ☹

\ [i·deal·i·za·tion] \

the narcissists inability to see a person as "many shades of grey", but instead as black or white, "good or bad.

*"**idealization** happens in phase one of the narcissistic cycle where the narcissist sees their newest target as perfect.*

idealization phase one   category: 💣✳   ☹

\ [i·deal·ized ◆ phase ◆ one] \

part one of the 3-part narcissistic cycle of abuse, where the narcissist idolizes the victim.

*"the goal of the **idealization phase one** is to get the victim under control of the narcissist.*

identify shift   category: ☹
\ [i·den·ti·ty ✦ shift] \

1: anything that pollutes or causes change in a person's entire being. 2: The loss or change of one's true identity.

*"When a victim suffers from a core **identify shift** they feel as though they are invisible.*

identify theft   category: 💣※
\ [i·den·ti·ty ✦ theft] \

when the narcissist erases the victim's "identity" by usurping or eclipsing what makes them a unique individual.

*"samples of narcissist **identity theft** is when the narcissist takes credit for another person's accomplishments or ideas, or steels other's limelight."*

impending doom   category: ☹
\ [im·pen·ding ✦ doom] \

an intense feeling that something terrible is going to happen, even though there's no apparent danger.

*"**impending doom** is a result of anxiety."*

individuation
category: ✿

\ [in·di·vi·u·a·tion] \

the process of forming an individual personality.

"the healing journey must include the victim reclaiming their individuation, which is lost during the degrading phase of abuse."

inner critic
category: ⊗

\ [in·ner ✦ cri·tic] \

(See pathological critic)

integrating behavior
category: 💣 ⊗

\ [in·te·gra·ting ✦ be·hav·ior] \

(narcissist definition) when the narcissist uses flattery to get on the good side of someone.

(victim definition) when the victim uses people pleasing behavior to get on someone's good side.

*"the narcissist can use integrating behavior when manipulating people for information or fuel. The victim can use **integrating behavior** when trying to avoid punishment or rejection."*

intellectual empathy
category: 💣

\ [in·tel·lect·tual ✦ em·path·y] \

when the narcissist reads the expressions of others to understand their emotions, or when they hear a description of how others feel and then has a rational response.

"it is not that a narcissist has empathy. They instead have intellectual empathy, as they are read their subjects for signs of emotion."

intermittent reinforcement   category:
\ [in·ter·mit·tent ✦ re·in·force·ment] \

an abuse pattern of behavior where the narcissist randomly intersperses acts of kindness between acts of cruelty.

"because the victim never knows when the narcissist will show kindness, the intermittent reinforcement, (a.k.a. random acts of benevolence) serves as one of the most critical forces that keeps the victim tied and addicted to the relationship."

intermittent explosive disorder   category: 💣☀
\ [in·ter·mit·tent ✦ ex·plo·sive ✦ dis·or·der] \

a disorder characterized by explosive outbursts of anger and violence in which one reacts out of proportion to the situation.

"with intermittent explosive disorder, the punishment never fits the crime."

internal guidance system   category: ✿
\ [in·ter·nal ✦ gui·dance ✦ sys·tem] \

also known as the internal g.p.s., the internal guidance system is our inner gut feeling that allows us to *feel* our way into wellness.

*"to heal, we must reconnect with our **internal guidance system** and learn to ask "How does this feel to me."*

invalidation   category:
\ [in·val·i·da·tion] \

a manipulative abuse tactic used by the narcissist to get the target to believe that their thoughts, opinions, and beliefs are wrong, unimportant or don't matter.

*"**invalidation** is a form of gaslighting."*

invert narcissist   category:
\ [in·vert ♦ nar·ci·ssist] \

a subtype of covert narcissism.

*"the **invert narcissist** is a codependent who craves to be in a relationship with a narcissist, regardless of the abuse inflicted on him or her."*

invisible child   category:
\ [in·vis·a·ble ♦ child] \

the child within the narcissistic family that is overlooked by the narcissist.

*"the **invisible child** is the one whose interests, emotions, needs, thoughts, and feelings are often devalued and discarded by the narcissist's neglect."*

invisible self
category: ☹

\ [in·vis·a·ble ◆ self] \

an identity crisis and trauma response where the victim feels unseen and unheard, i.e., invisible.

"the invisible self happens when the victim is not seen or accepted for who they really are."

irritable male syndrome
category: 💣※

\ [ir·rit·a·ble ◆ male ◆ syn·drome] \

(See Jekyll Hyde syndrome)

is factor
category: ✿

\ [is ◆ fac·tor] \

a recovery term where the survivor learns to stop taking the actions of the narcissist personal by putting it in a neutral zone.

"the goal of the "is factor" is to remove all emotion from within the narcissistic relationship and accept the condition, situation, and behaviors of the narcissist as "it is what it is."

isolation
category: 💣※

\ [i·so·la tion] \

a technique the narcissist uses to isolate the victim from the outside world.

"the goal of isolation is to keep the victim from outside influences so the narcissist can gain control."

J

jokasti syndrome   category: ☹
\ [jo·kas·ti ✦ syn·drom] \

a syndrome found within narcissistic parenting
where the narcissist has incestuous sexual
desires towards their child.

*"most **jokasti syndrome** cases involve a narcissistic mother
whose focus / target is her Golden Child son."*

jekyll hyde syndrome   category: ☹
\ [jek·yll ✦ hyde ✦ syn·drome] \

a personality disorder known as Split Personality
Disorder where the carrier can go from nice to
awful without warning.

*"one of the first recognizable signs that a narcissistic
relationship is shifting into phase two is when the narcissist
shows signs of **Jekyll Hyde** behavior, where his or her
personality starts to become unpredictable."*

K

kool aid syndrome
category: ☹

\ [learned ◆ help·less·ness] \

also known as "drinking the kool-aid", this term describes anyone who is under the "influence" and control of the narcissist.

*"from a blind victim to flying monkeys, anyone who subscribes to the reality of the narcissist truly as drank the **kool-aid**."*

L

learned helplessness   category: ☹
\ [learned ♦ help·less·ness] \

a trauma wound that occurs after chronic abuse,
where the victim develops passive resignation.
*"much like an elephant tied to a plastic chair feels helpless
to the small chain that binds it, **learned helplessness**
happens to narcissistic abuse victims where they "lose their
power" after mental conditioning and "put downs" that
erodes the victim's self-worth."*

linen cupboard syndrome   category: ☹
\ [lin·en ♦ cup·board ♦ syn·drome] \

a term related to trauma memories where the
victim can only see emotional clutter when trying
to remember what happened.
*"taken from the movie The Cabinet of Dr. Caligari, the **linen
cupboard syndrome** happens to most abuse victims when
trying to recount the trauma."*

lost child syndrome   category: ☹
\ [lost ♦ child ♦ syn·drome] \

a child within the narcissistic family who copes
with the family trauma by staying under the radar,

and by making few demands.
"most lost children in a narcissistic family have a very difficult time asking for help."

love addiction   category: ☹
\ [love • a·ddic·tion] \

a process addiction (i.e., an addiction that doesn't involve drugs or alcohol), that rather than the person being addicted do drugs, they are instead addicted to a person or love interest, where this love interest like any addiction, seems impossible for the victim to leave.

"love addiction and its behaviors are as dangerous and detrimental to one's life as is a drug."

love bombing   category: 💣✳
\ [love • bomb·ing] \

a narcissistic abuse technique where the narcissist uses intense positive attention to create an intense bond with the victim, so he or she will become vulnerable to, trusting of, and dependent on the narcissist.

"love bombing can include behaviors such as excessive flattery and declarations of love, mirroring, future-faking, gifts, sex, domination of the partner's time, and fast-tracking the relationship."

low contact
category: ☼

\ [low • con·tact] \

the amount of identified limited time you consciously choose to spend with the narcissist to keep yourself safe and healthy.

"when no contact is not an option, professionals recommend low contact."

M

madonna complex   category: ☹
\ [ma·donna ◆ com·plex] \

the inability to maintain sexual arousal within a
committed, loving relationship.
*"when the narcissist began sexually abandoning the
relationship, rather than recognize it as the narcissistic
Madonna complex, she took it personal."*

magical thinking   category: ☹
\ [ma·gi·cal ◆ think·ing] \

a thinking process where the victim believes that
the narcissist will "magically" change.
"magical thinking is a sign of codependence."

malign return   category: 💣
\ [ma·ligne ◆ re·turn] \

a form of narcissistic abuse that happens post–
relationship, where the narcissist commits to a long–
term season of trying to destroy the victim.
*"the abuse did not end when he left. Instead, a season of
malign return began, that lasted a year."*

malignant narcissist
category:

\ [ma·lig·nant ✦ nar·ci·ssist] \

an unofficial term that describes the type of
narcissism that is in the middle of the narcissistic
spectrum.

*"it was difficult to recognize the full extent of his/her
narcissism because he/she was a **malignant narcissist** and
therefore at times displayed normal behavior."*

marginalizing:
category:

\ [mar·gin·al·i·zing] \

an abuse technique where the narcissist
undermines others so they can stay superior.

*"examples of narcissistic **marginalizing** includes nitpicking,
judging, criticizing, comparing and invalidating the
successes or the emotions of those who threaten the
narcissist."*

mascot
category: ☹

\ [mas·cot] \

the child in the narcissistic family who plays the
cute or funny "jester" role.

*"the **mascot** child uses humor to diffuse the family
tensions."*

mask
category: 💣✳
\ [mask] \

also known as masking, it is the different faces the narcissist shows in public or to those he or she wants to impress.

*"it is common for a narcissist to put on a **mask** to strangers and yet show their family their true colors."*

mask slipping
category: 💣✳
\ [mask ✦ slip·ping] \

when the "front" or "mask of sanity' the narcissist presents to people begins to slip, it is called "mask slipping."

*"there was an obvious shift in her/his behavior when the **mask began to slip**, and we started seeing true colors."*

mean and sweet cycle
category: 💣✳
\ [mean ✦ and ✦ sweet ✦ cy·cle] \
(See bait and switch)

megalomaniac
category: 💣✳
\ [meg·lo·man·i·ac] \

a narcissist who believes that he or she has unlimited power or importance.

*"you see many **megalomaniacs** in politics."*

mental abuse   category:
\ [mental • a·buse] \

(See emotional abuse)

mental disorder   category:
\ [mental • dis·order] \

a disorder that causes psychological and behavioral
disturbances with varying severities.
*"narcissistic personality disorder is a **mental disorder**."*

minimalizing   category:
\ [min·i·mil·i·zing] \

an abuse tactic and a form of control where the
narcissist will minimize others' ideas, successes,
positions, thoughts, or possessions to keep their
overinflated image of themselves intact.
*"in all the years I knew her, she never had anything nice to say
about anyone, and was constantly **minimalizing** everyone, even
her own sister."*

mirroring   category:
\ [mirror·ing] \

a narcissistic tactic used during phase one in the
narcissistic cycle of abuse where the narcissist
mimics the partner's body language, behaviors,

speech style, and actions. It can also occur when the narcissist claims to enjoy the same activities as the target or to have had similar experiences to make it appear as if the two have a lot in common.

*"the goal of **mirroring** is for the target to believe she and the narcissist have a lot in common. It is part of the conditioning phase."*

misdirected anger
category:

\ [mis·di·rec·ted ✦ an·ger] \

a by-proxy form of abuse where the victim of narcissistic trauma takes out their anger and / or retaliates against an innocent party, because the victim has not properly dealt with his or her own anger.

*"unfortunately, due to the victim's **misdirected anger** many began to believe she had become the narcissist."*

moving the goal post
category:

\ [mov·ing ✦ the ✦ goal ✦ post] \

an abuse and control tactic where the narcissist continually changes the desired outcome and expectations of the target.

*"the reason the narcissist **moves the goal post** is to ensure that the narcissist can be constantly dissatisfied with the victim. The chronic "failing" of the victim and the*

*frustration or continued chasing to get it right serves as a
fuel source for the narcissist."*

moving the start line
category:
\ [mov·ing ◆ the ◆ start ◆ line] \

an abuse and control tactic where the narcissist
continually sets new "start-over" dates after they
make a mistake.

*"the goal of **moving the start line** is so the narcissist can
avoid any accountability or consequences to their mistake."*

mr / ms breathy
category:
\ [mr / ms ◆ breath·y] \

a manipulation and control tactic where the
narcissist speaks in a weak / "breathy "voice
tone, and one word answers to notify the victim
that they have injured or disappointed the
narcissist.

*"an example of **Mr. or Ms. Breathy** is when the target asks
the narcissist, "What is wrong?" and the narcissist responds
with a breathy, '···Nothing···"*

mr / ms long face
category:
\ [mr / ms ◆ long ◆ face] \

a manipulation and control tactic where the
narcissist will visually pout with a sad or

discontent expression so the target will understand they have disappointed the narcissist.

*"rather than use direct communication, the narcissist instead uses passive aggressive, covert communication with **Mr. or Ms long face** to express their disappointment."*

mr / ms opposite
category:

\ [mr / ms ◆ op·po·sit] \

a manipulation and control tactic where the narcissist will intentionally take the opposite view or position of the victim to make the victim feel rejected and less than.

*"**Mr. or Ms. Opposite** is an intentional act of gaslighting against the victim."*

my way or the highway syndrome
category:

\ [my ◆ way ◆ or ◆ the ◆ high·way] \

a control tactic where the narcissist demands full agreement from the victim.

*"if the victim does not align with the narcissist's **"my way out the highway"** mentality, abandonment, threat or harm will ensue.*

mythical thinking   category: 💣✳

\ [my·thi·cal • think·ing] \

the thinking process of the narcissist where they believe they are the best, can do no wrong, or have no adverse consequences to their actions.

*"part of the problem is the narcissist believes their **mythical thinking**."*

N

narcissist   category: 💣※

\ [nar·ci·sist] \

a self-centered personality style, characterized as
having an excessive interest in one's physical
appearance and an excessive pre-occupation with
one's own needs, often at the expense of others.
pathological self-absorption.

*"the term **narcissist** was first identified as a mental
disorder by the British essayist and physician Havelock Ellis
in 1898."*

narcanese   category: 💣※

\[nar·can·ese]\

the non-official "language" of the narcissist that
includes both spoken and written word as well as
behaviors, beliefs and tactics that he or she uses
while in an episode, to try to dupe or gain control
of others.

*"healing happens when you learn to speak **narcanese**."*

narcissistic abuse cycle   category: ✿
\ [nar·ci·sis·tic ✦ a·buse ✦ cy·cle] \

the predictable cycle of abuse the narcissist
implements on the victim.
*'different than the traditional abuse cycle, the **Narcissistic**
Abuse Cycle has three phases. 1: The Golden Stage (also
known as the Idealization or Dream Girl / Boy phase) 2: The
Devaluation phase and 3: the Discard phase."*

narcissistic abuse syndrome   category: ☹
\ [nar·ci·sis·tic ✦ a·buse ✦ syn·drome] \

a serious condition that displays a cluster of
symptoms that results after a person experiences a
relationship with a person suffering from high
narcissistic tendencies, narcissistic personality
disorder, or anti-social personality disorder.
*"**narcissistic abuse syndrome** requires specific healing for the
victim to fully recover."*

narcissistic brain damage   category: ☹
\ [nar·ci·sis·tic ✦ brain ✦ dam·age] \

(see abuse amnesia)

narcissistic branding   category: 💣☀ ☹
\ [nar·ci·sis·tic ✦ brand·ing] \

when the narcissist insists their target brand

themselves with a tattoo or other permanent mark
to prove their love and loyalty.
*"thank God for laser, as she got rid of the **narcissistic branding**
out of pressure."*

narcissistic bubble

category:

\ [nar·ci·sis·tic ✦ bu·ble] \

the self-validating bubble the narcissist forms
where overtime causes them to lose their sense of
accountability for their behavior.
*"he lived in a **narcissistic bubble** that was impenetrable."*

narcissistic collapse

category:

\ [nar·ci·sis·tic ✦ co·llapse] \

a psychological breakdown that happens when
someone with narcissistic personality disorder
(NPD) can no longer uphold their grandiose,
confident image.
*"as a narcissist feels profoundly threatened, when he or she
can no longer control the situation via rage and lashing out
they will often fall into a **narcissistic collapse**. That is when
we see how truly weak they are.*

narcissistic conditioning   category:
\ [nar·ci·sis·tic ◆ con·di·tion·ing] \

the process where the narcissist uses manipulative
behavior and slowly "conditions" the target to adopt
radically different beliefs from their own.

*"the goal of narcissistic conditioning is for the victim to become
the primary fuel source of the narcissist."*

narcissistic consumption   category:
\ [nar·ci·sis·tic ◆ con·sump·tion] \

a form of conspicuous consumption where the
narcissist seeks products that help them enhance
their self−worth and self−importance.

*"there are four speculated reasons for **narcissistic
consumption**. 1: the desire for individuation (being unique
or different) and elevation (feeling privileged or of higher
social rank). 2: materialism, i.e., symbolic product purchases
indicate the financial success, wealth accumulation, and
power of the narcissist. 3: the pursuit of meaning in life, i.e.,
symbolic purchases contribute to the perception that life for
the narcissist has significance and purpose. 4: sexual
signaling, i.e., symbolic product purchasing tends to
increase the consumer's sexual appeal.*

narcissistic environment   category:
\ [nar·ci·sis·tic ♦ en·vi ron ment] \

any environment that is being governed by
narcissism.

*"the family was paralyzed because their home was clearly
they were raised in a **narcissistic environment**."*

narcissistic envy   category:
\ [nar·ci·sis·tic ♦ en·vy] \

the intense envy and jealousy the narcissist feels
towards others.

*"**narcissistic envy** drives a narcissist to 'steal' (figuratively)
portions of another person's status, respect, or sympathy. It
usually harms the person they morally robbed."*

narcissistic family system   category:
\ [nar·ci·sis·tic ♦ fam·i·ly ♦ sys·tem] \

a family that is led by a powerful parent with a
narcissistic personality disorder, and the result it
has on both the specific roles each child plays
and how they are treated.
(See Golden Child, Lost Child, Scapegoat Child
and Mascot Child for more.)

*"nothing but trauma comes from a **narcissistic family
system**."*

narcissistic fatigue
category: ☹

\ [nar·ci·sis·tic ◆ fa·ti·gue] \

a form of physical, emotional, mental, and
psychological maladies (illnesses) that stem from
the stress experienced from prolong exposure to
chronic narcissistic abuse.

*"she had a chronic case of dizziness that was later
diagnosed as **narcissistic fatigue**."*

narcissistic filter
category:

\ [nar·ci·sis·tic ◆ fil·ter] \

the perspective of a person who can only process
information according to how he or she sees the
world.

*"the narcissist cannot listen to another point of view
because of their **narcissistic filter**."*

narcissistic induced depression
category: ☹

\ [nar·ci·sis·tic ◆ in·duced ◆ de·pres·sion] \

an onset of depression specifically caused by
enduring a narcissistic episode.

*"she was overjoyed to learn that her depression was
classified as **narcissistic induced depression** as it only
affected her after a narcissistic episode."*

narcissistic induced fear
category:
\ [nar·ci·sis·tic ✦ in·duced ✦ fear] \

a term used to describe the intense fear the
narcissist puts on the victim to extract fuel.
*"she was consumed with fear not because of reality, but
because of the **narcissistic induced fear** he was drilling into
her."*

narcissistic injury
category:
\ [nar·ci·sis·tic ✦ in·ju·y] \

a psychological term used to describe an emotional
"injury to the ego" that the narcissist experiences
when the victim or anyone else, does something to
criticize, threaten or attack the narcissist's idealized
"perfect" self-image that he or she has of himself or
herself.
*"**narcissistic injuries,** more often than not, require retaliation
from the narcissist."*

narcissistic mind reading
category:
\ [nar·ci·sis·tic ✦ mind ✦ read·ing] \

1: a delusional expectation where the narcissist
believes the victim or others, are to have the
power to "read their mind" and know every detail
and need about them without them having to say
anything. 2: when the narcissist believes they

know what you are thinking.

"it is important to remember that there is no such thing as **narcissistic mind reading.** *No person has the ability or the responsibility to read minds."*

narcissistic mortification
category:
\ [nar·ci·sis·tic ✦ mor·ti·fi·ca·tion] \

known as "death by embarrassment." Defined by Sigmond Freud, it is the intense fear associated with narcissistic injury and humiliation.

"the narcissist was consumed with **narcissistic mortification** *when he / she realized their true colors were exposed."*

narcissistic nit-picking
category:
\ [nar·ci·sis·tic ✦ nit·pick·ing] \

an abuse technique where the narcissist will covertly abuse the victim by lightly but consistently nit–picking, fault–finding, taking the opposite opinion, and/or acting irritated towards their victim until they see them begin to deteriorate.

"the goal of **narcissistic nit-picking** *is to covertly extract fuel supply without the victim recognizing the nit–picking as abuse."*

narcissistic perfectionism
category:
\ [nar·ci·sis·tic ✦ per·fec·tion·ism] \

(see abusive expectations)

narcissistic personality disorder (npd) category: ⚙
\ [nar·ci·sis·tic ✦ per·son·al·I ·ty ✦ dis·or·der] \

a type of personality disorder within the Cluster B category characterized by the following impairments: overreliance on others for self-definition; overreliance on others for regulation of self-esteem; lack of empathy; exploitative of others; grandiose delusions; exaggerated entitlement; excessive attention seeking; and excessive admiration seeking.

*"people with **narcissistic personality disorder** depend emotionally on others to sustain their sense of identity and regulate their self-esteem. These individuals typically suffer invalidating emotional injury during their early years that interferes with the healthy development of a stable identify, a sense of self-esteem, and emotional empathy."*

narcissistic projection   category:
\ [nar·ci·sis·tic ✦ pro·jec·tion] \

when a narcissist "tells on themselves" by projecting, accusing, or pointing out faults in their victim that are actually their own character flaws, bad behaviors, ill intentions, and accusations.

*"the narcissist kept telling her that she was selfish, but in truth the narcissist was just **projecting**."*

narcissistic rage   category: 💣✳

\ [nar·ci·sis·tic ✦ rage] \

a technical term to describe the blind anger and
rage the narcissist displays when their shame is
triggered due to a narcissistic injury. It can include
acts of revenge to acts of violence.

"*narcissistic rage is terrifying, sometimes physically
violent, and far beyond normal anger as the punishment
never fits the crime. Narcissistic rage is emotionally and
physically traumatizing for those on the receiving end,
particularly children, who naturally blame themselves for
adults' reactions.*"

narcissistic spectrum   category: ⚙

\ [nar·ci·sis·tic ✦ spec·trum] \

a scale of 0–10 that governs whether a person
has a little sense of self-importance, or a
narcissistic personality disorder.

"*the narcissistic spectrum has six markers: Self-Love
Deficiency Disorder -> Healthy Narcissism -> Narcissistic
Tendencies / Characteristics -> Narcissistic Personality
Disorder -> Sociopath -> Psychopath.*"

narcissistic storms   category: 💣✳

\ [nar·ci·sis·tic ✦ storms] \

the predictable abuses the victim encounters after
they start to set boundaries with the narcissist.

*"much like a weather report can predict the direction of a storm, **narcissists storms** are also predictable, victims therefore can protect themselves from the predictable narcissistic "storms" of abuses.*

narcissistic supply   category:
\ [nar·ci·sis·tic ✦ sup·ply] \

a process and excessive need where the narcissist uses people and situations to self-medicate their self-esteem and keep their "specialness" intact. They do this by extracting attention, adoration, admiration, and support from their targets. There are three primary levels of fuel for the narcissist: primary resource, secondary resource, and tertiary resource.

*"without **narcissistic supply**, the narcissist feels they might die or dissipate."*

narcissistic tendencies   category: ✿
\ [nar·ci·sis·tic ✦ ten·den·cies] \

also known as narcissistic characteristics, it is a marker on the narcissistic spectrum that identifies a person who does not have Narcissistic Personality Disorder but has many thought, behaviors and beliefs found within narcissistic behavior.

*"people with **narcissistic tendencies** tend to be very difficult people and can cause as much trauma as a person with NPD."*

narcissistic trigger   category:
\ [nar·ci·sis·tic ♦ trig·ger] \
> also known as narcissistic characteristics, it is a
> marker on the narcissistic spectrum that identifies a
> person who does not have Narcissistic Personality

narcissistic victim syndrome   category:
\ [nar·ci·sis·tic ♦ vic·tim ♦ syn·drome] \
> (see narcissistic abuse syndrome)

narcissistic view finder   category:
\ [nar·ci·sis·tic ♦ view ♦ finders] \
> the pinpoint ability (or lack thereof) the narcissist
> views life through.
> *"the narcissist views life through a **narcissistic view finder**.
> That is why their thinking is so limited."*

narkie-ville   category:
\[nar·kie ♦ ville]\
> the non-official word to describe the insane world
> of the narcissist that has its own governing laws,
> its own judicial, prison and punishment system,
> and a language of its own.
> *"**narkie-ville** might not be on the map, but it is real."*

neglect
category: 💣※

\ [ne ⬧ glect] \

a passive form of abuse in which the narcissist ignores the emotional, psychological, and/or physical needs of their partner or children.

"neglect can range from not providing adequate food or shelter, to failing to provide affection, supervision, or protection or appropriate sexual touch."

nice to nasty cycle
category: 💣※

\ [nas·ty ⬧ to ⬧ nice ⬧ cy·cle] \

(see bait and switch)

no contact
category: ✿

\ [no ⬧ con·tact] \

the process where the victim of narcissistic abuse chooses to end all contact with the narcissist.

"for adult children of narcissists, no contact is typically a deeply ambivalent and painful choice that feels like a matter of survival to break the cycle of hurt and to attempt to heal."

non-negotiables
category: ✿

\ [non·ne·go·tia·bles] \

a set of healthy needs the survivor has that he or she refuses to "negotiate."

"non-negotiables include such things as safety, dreams, finances, peace, privacy, authentic love, clarity, the right to

be human, the right to dialogue, respect, reciprocity,
environments, treatment, value, and self-love."

non-productive arguments   category:
\ [non·pro·duc·tive ✦ ar·gu·ments] \

(see fights over nothing)

non-validation   category:
\ [non·val·i·da·tion] \

an abusive technique where the narcissist refuses
to validate the emotions of the victim for the
trauma they caused.

*"the narcissist wants to believe that the **non-validation**
means the abuse never happened. But that is a lie."*

normalizing   category:
\ [nor·mal·i·zing] \

a survival response of the victim who after
chronic narcissistic abuse loses the ability to
sense the danger of the narcissist.

*'the abuse had become so **normalized** that she saw the
drastic or dangerous acts of the narcissist as a 'normal'
human response."*

O

object constancy   category:
\ [ob·ject ♦ con·stan·cy] \

a condition where the narcissist lacks the ability to
have both positive thoughts and negative thoughts
towards the same person who they are
disappointed or hurt by.

*"when triggered, the narcissist's **object continuity** of
perception collapses into present-moment reactive emotion.
For example, if his/her child forgets to do a chore, the
narcissist father may become enraged and punish him/her,
seeing the behavior as spiteful or irresponsible even if the
child is usually conscientious."*

observe don't absorb system   category: ✿
\ [ob·serve ♦ don't ♦ ab·sorb] \

a recovery technique that when the narcissist
tries to get you in an emotional "wrestling match"
you consciously choose to detach or step back
from the abuse and observe their manipulative
techniques for what they are, but not own them,
by not engaging.

*"One tool in recovery is the "**observe don't absorb**
technique" where the victim forms an emotional acrylic wall
between them and the narcissist's actions, thereby not*

allowing their energy to penetrate their mind, soul or emotions."

out of integrity   category: ☹
\ [out • of • in·te·grity] \

a side effect of narcissistic abuse where the victim has lost the trust of one's own value system.
"when we step out of our healing, we step out of integrity, of ourself."

overt narcissist   category: 💣
\ [o·vert • nar·ci·ssist] \

a "garden–variety" or typical definition of a narcissist whose emotional displays, grandiosity and feelings of entitlement and superiority are on obvious display to others.
"overt narcissist are easy to spot. These individuals are larger–than–life, arrogant, often loud, and boisterous; they love to be the center of attention, and often come across as obnoxious to most people."

P

parasite
category:

\ [pa·ra·site] \

a word used to describe the behavior of the narcissist, who "attaches" him or herself to a person.

*"just as a **parasite** attaches itself to an object for survival, the narcissist becomes a parasite to his or her target."*

parental alienation syndrome
category:

\ [par·en·tal ✦ a·li·en·a·tion ✦ syn·drome] \

a term that describes what happens to the child when one parent attempts to turn the children against the other parent.

*"in my opinion, **parental alienation** is a form of child abuse."*

parentification
category:

\ [paren·ti·fi·ca·tion] \

a role reversal whereby a parent inappropriately looks to a child to take on parental roles and responsibilities in the family.

*"clearly, the **parentification** created huge trauma on the child who was expected to meet the emotional, physical, and/or sexual needs of the narcissistic parent."*

pathological critic

category:

\ [path·o·lo·gi·cal • cri·tic] \

a term coined by psychologist Eugene Sagan, to describe the negative inner voice that attacks and judges a person from within.

*"everyone has a critical inner voice, but those people with negative self-appraisal tend to have a more vicious and vocal **pathological** critic.*

pathological lying

category:

\ [path·o·lo·gi·cal • ly·ing] \

lying that is done compulsively out of habit.

*"you could not trust a word she said as she was a **pathological** liar."*

pawn

category:

\ [pawn] \

close and dedicated friends who believe the narcissist is amazing, but who the narcissist is using only to do their dirty work or supply them fuel.

*"she thought they were friends, but she was only the narcissist's **pawn**."*

pedestal
category:

\ [ped·es·tal] \

the glorified position where the narcissist elevates
the target to "perfect."

*"the narcissist places his or her target is on **pedestal** during
the golden period when both the victim and the narcissist
see each other as amazing."*

personality disorder
category: ✿

\ [per·son·ality • dis·or·der] \

a diagnosis found in the DSM that describes
deeply ingrained and maladaptive pattern of
behavior, that typically manifests by the time one
reaches adolescence and causing long term
difficulties in personal relationships or functioning
in society.

*"people are not born with a **personality disorder**; it is
formed over years and years of dysfunction."*

physical abuse
category:

\ [phy·si·cal • a·buse] \

any intentional act causing injury or trauma to
another person or animal by way of bodily
contact.

*"also know as physical assault or physical violence, **physical
abuse** is crime punishable by law."*

playbook
category:

\ [play·book] \

a mental document the narcissist creates where he or she collects information on the target and then implements various narcissistic techniques towards that person.

*"every narcissist has a **playbook** that is filled with the manipulations they use against people to get fuel."*

pink cloud syndrome
category: ⚙

\ [pink ◆ cloud ◆ syn·drome] \

(aka "pink clouding") a recovery term used to describe the feeling of elation many narcissistic abuse survivors feel shortly after getting away from their abuser.

*"though she had a lot of healing to do, there was no doubt she was riding high on the **pink cloud syndrome**."*

pitch forking
category:

\ [pitch ◆ fork·ing] \

a technique the narcissist uses where they will say and do things to find the victim's tender spots or breaking points, so they can obtain narcissistic fuel.

*"he continued **pitch forking** her until he found her tender spot; then we went in for the emotional kill."*

plausible denial   category: 💣✳

\ [plau·si·ble ♦ de·ni·a·bil·ity] \

a technique the narcissist uses when they carefully select every word to create deniability.

"*examples of* **plausible denial** *include statements such as, "I am not having sex with that person." To the narcissist this means "at this very moment, I am not having sex with that person."*"

poop in your soup   category: ✿

\ [poop ♦ in ♦ your ♦ soup] \

a term developed by Dana Morningstar that emphasizes that even the smallest amount of narcissistic abuse is unacceptable.

"*any amount of narcissism is like* **poop in your soup**, *and even the smallest piece of poop in your soup is never okay!*"

polarized thinking   category: 💣✳☹

\ [pol·ar·ized ♦ think·ing] \

(see black and white thinking)

post abuse cycle of despair   category: 💣✳☹

\ [post ♦ a·buse ♦ cy·cle ♦ of ♦ dis·pair] \

a term coined by Dr. Tracy that describes the cycle an abuse victim processes through after a narcissistic episode leaves him or her in physical and or psychological shock.

*"there are 6 stages in the post abuse cycle of despair.
Daze -> Anxiety-> Depression -> Despair -> Anger_>
Physical Illness. (For more, see The Courage to Say No
More, found on Amazon)*

prediction and preparation   category: ✿
\[pre·dic·tion ✦ and ✦ pre·par·a·tion] \

(see anticipated losses)

present time living   category: ✿
\[pre·sent ✦ time ✦ liv·ing] \

a recovery word that describes the ability to be
aware of each situation you are in and make
choices based on that present moment.

*"part of healing from CPTSD and the anxiety it causes is to
stay in **present time living**."*

projection   category: 💣✳
\[pro·jec·tion] \

(see narcissistic projection)

predictive awareness   category: ✿
\[pre·dic·tive ✦ a·ware·ness] \

a recovery tool where the victim clearly
understands the characteristics of narcissism and as

a result is able to protection him or herself.

*"the book Love and War that describes **predictive awareness** as, "If you know your enemies and know yourself, you will not be imperiled in 100 battles. If you do not know your enemies but know yourself, you will win one and lose on. If you do not know your enemies and do not know yourself, you will lose every battle."*

primary resource   category:
\ [pri·mar·y ✦ re·source] \

level one in the three-tier fuel narcissistic fuel source supply chain.

*"the **primary resource** is the main person the narcissist extracts fuel from. This is typically a mate, family member or children."*

private shaming   category:
\ [pri·vat ✦ sham·ing] \

also known as secret shaming, a form of abuse where the narcissist shames the target in covert ways.

*"examples of **private shaming** include behind closed doors shame campaigns, muttered comments, and passive aggressive non-verbals. The goal is to alienate the victim with shame."*

psychic virus
category:
\ [psy·chic ✦ vi·rus] \

a term developed by Melanie Tonia that describes how the toxicity of narcissistic abuse affects the victim physically and psychologically.

*"just as a physical virus can make you physically ill, narcissistic abuse creates a **psychic virus** where the symptoms include words that burn holes in the soul; memories that cause nightmares; and a long term toxic connection that can only be healed through professional help."*

psychopath
category:
\ [psy·cho·path] \

though not a specific diagnosis found in the DSM, it is a term on the narcissistic spectrum to describe a narcissist who lacks a conscience, and has the ability to intentionally, with pre-thought, manipulate and deceive without or remorse.

*"the term **psychopath** is recognized by the DSM-5-TR and is considered more biological than environmental. People with psychopathy are very dangerous people."*

public shaming
category:
\ [pub·lic ✦ sham·ing] \

also known as public humiliation, it is a form of abuse where the narcissist will dishonor or disgrace the victim in a public place or in front of others.

*"he specifically chose **public shaming** because he knew she would not fight back in front of others."*

R

rage disorder
category:
\ [rage ◆ dis·order] \
(see intermittent explosive disorder.)

reactive anger
category:
\ [re·ac·tive ◆ an·ger] \
an aggressive form of anger displayed by the
victim of narcissistic abuse, after provoked by the
narcissist.
*"the narcissist would provoke the victim into **reactive anger**,
then call her/him "insane" for her response."*

recharge
category:
\ [re·charge] \
an abuse technique where the narcissist, when
feeling low on fuel, will return to a fuel source to
"recharge" him or herself.
*"it is not that the narcissist missed her and needed her love;
he needed a recharge to **recharge** his ego."*

reciprocity
category: ✿
\ [re·ci·pro·ci·ty] \
a recovery term where the survivor of narcissistic

abuse learns the practice of exchanging things with others, for *mutual* benefit.

*"examples of **reciprocity** include exchanging love for love and respect for respect."*

reality check   category: ✿

\ [re·al·ity • check] \

the awareness and recovery tool where the victim accepts that one's physical well-being is the responsibility of oneself.

*"healing requires a person to learn the skill of **reality checks** and the responsibility of being responsible for where you are and how people are treating you."*

reality warping   category:

\ [re·al·ity • warp·ing] \

a control technique where the narcissist warps the reality of what was said or done.

*"**reality warping** is a form of gaslighting where for example the narcissist will say, "I know I said it, but it is not true.""*

redefining   category:

\ [re·de·fin·ing] \

also known as "reshaping reality," this is an abuse technique where the narcissist will recreate the narrative to fit their need or story.

*"the goal of **redefining** (reality) is to justify that what the*

narcissist is doing is "good" and what they are saying is
"right", even though it is not."

resigned passiveness   category: ☹
\ [re·signed • pass·ive·ness] \

a trauma response that happens when a victim of
narcissistic abuse reaches a point of learned
helplessness due to ongoing drenching of
emotional sabotage.

"she slipped into **resigned passiveness** *because she was*
beaten down due to the years of abuse."

resolution   category: ✿
\ [re·so·lu·tion] \

a recovery word that describes the action of
solving a problem, dispute, or contentious matter.

"narcissists cannot allow for **resolution***, as resolution*
creates peace; and peace does not provide fuel."

respite   category: ☹
\[re·spite] \

a term that describes a short period of rest or
relief from something difficult or unpleasant.

"in the narcissistic abuse cycle, **respite** *describes those*
moments of calm before the storm."

righteous anger
category: ⚙
\ [right·eous ◆ an·ger] \

also known as healthy anger, righteous anger is a
reactive emotion of anger, over perceived
mistreatment, insult, or malice of another.
"reactive anger is part of the grief cycle."

rumination
category:
\ [rum·in·na·tion] \

a trauma abuse syndrome where the victim of
narcissistic abuse is unable to stop thinking about,
or is chronically searching for, how they can fix
the problem and why it happened in the first
place.
*"the narcissist wants the victim to **ruminate**, as they extract
fuel from the idea that their target is relentlessly thinking
about them."*

S

safe and sacred place
category:

\ [safe ◆ and sac·red ◆ place] \

a recovery term to describe the "time and location" a person in recovery sets aside each day to process the anger and pain issues.

*"one of the most important healing habits is to form your own **safe and sacred place**."*

sadistic narcissist
category:

\[sa·dis·tic ◆ nar·cis·sist] \

a narcissist who obtains pleasure from inflicting pain on others.

*"he was obviously a **sadistic narcissist** as he actually received pleasure watching me cry."*

sanctuary wounds
category: ☹

\[sanc·tu·ar·y ◆ wounds] \

a recovery term to describe the deep trauma wounds that happen on account of someone you love or trusted, versus a stranger or acquaintance.

*"part of the healing journey is to directly face the **sanctuary wounds** we experienced, as if we don't it can taint our understanding of love for the rest of our life."*

scapegoat   category:
\[scape·goat] \

a term that describes the child in a narcissistic
family who is blamed for everything that goes
wrong. Scapegoats are typically blamed for
family problems, disciplined, or punished
disproportionately, burdened with excessive
chores and responsibilities, and subjected to
unmerited negative treatment.

*"the **scapegoat** child is the object of the narcissistic parent's
negative projections. He or she is devalued and treated as
an insignificant loser who is blamed for everything that goes
wrong, including things that are clearly the fault of others."*

scorecard   category:
\[score·card] \

an abuse tactic where the narcissist constantly
"keeps score" on how good they are, and how "not
good" the target is.

*"in love, there is no **scorecard**."*

segmented love   category:
\[seg·men·ted • love] \

an abuse tactic where the narcissist does not accept
the victim in his or her entirety, but instead will
"love" one aspect and "abhor" other parts.

*"the purpose of **segmented love** is to make the victim feel flawed and not enough."*

self-esteem   category: ✿
\ [self ✦ es·teem] \

the overall judgement one holds about their own self-worth

*"samples of **self-esteem** include the healthy pride in oneself, self-respect, self-efficacy and self-assurance."*

self-love   category: ✿
\ [self ✦ love] \

the conscious relationship one has with oneself that sets the tone for self-respect, value and worth.

*"**self-love** is a non-negotiable, not just in recovery, but in all areas of life."*

self-love deficiency disorder   category: ☹
\ [self ✦ love ✦ de·fi·cien·cy ✦ dis·order] \

a psychological term founded by Ross Rosenburg which describes the lack of self-love due to childhood trauma.

*"on the narcissism spectrum, **self-love deficiency disorder** is at the opposite end of narcissistic personality disorder; therefore recovery from narcissistic abuse trauma requires a victim to heal and repair the SLDD."*

self-love foundation   category: ✿
\ [self • love • foun·da·tion] \

a combination of beliefs, principles and tools that creates the infrastructure of one's self-love system.

*"we must all have a steely **self-love foundation**. It is the basis of healing."*

self-partnering   category: ✿
\ [self·part·ner·ing] \

a recovery term that means to empower yourself by loving yourself.

*"examples of **self-partnering** include giving yourself gifts, treating yourself like a friend, listening to your own feelings, dealing with your own fears, eliminating the need for approval, facing the fear of loneliness, looking deeper at your motivations, and finding which are helping and which are ego."*

self-regulating   category: ✿
\ [self • reg·u·la·ting] \

a recovery tool where the victim of narcissistic abuse gains the skills to regulate their emotions without intervention from external people.

*"one sign of personal power is the ability to **self-regulate**, especially after an encounter with the narcissist."*

self-soothing
category: ☼

\ [self ✦ sooth·ing] \

(see self-regulating)

secondary resource
category:

\ [se·con·dar·y ✦ re·source] \

the second level of fuel sourcing for the
narcissist.

*"a **secondary resource** for the narcissist includes the
narcissist's flying monkeys, the worshippers, the affairs,
new friends and lovers."*

sexual harassment
category:

\ [sex·u·al ✦ har·ass·ment] \

when the narcissist approaches the victim with
unwelcome sexual advances.

*"examples of **sexual harassment** include unwanted sexual
comments, written documents of explicit sex, or any sexual
act where the victim says no."*

secret shaming
category:

\ [se·cret ✦ sham·ing] \

(see private shaming)

self-care
category: ☼

\ [self ♦ care] \

the act of taking a conscious role in protecting one's own well-being and happiness, especially during periods of stress.

*"we cannot heal our esteem if we neglect our **self-care**."*

self-rescue
category: ☼

\ [self ♦ res·cue] \

1: the awareness and tool where the victim of narcissistic abuse accepts that one's physical well-being is the responsibility of oneself.

*"she truly **self-rescued** when she no longer needed the narcissist to change to begin healing."*

shame dumping
category:

\ [shame ♦ dump·ing] \

also known as shame shedding, this is an abusive technique the narcissist uses on the victim when the narcissist is being held accountable for a wrong action.

*"the purpose of the **shame dumping** is to shift the focus and blame off the narcissist and redirect it to the victim so the narcissist remains in control."*

shape shifting
\ [shame • shift·ing] \

category:

an abuse survival technique where the victim of
abuse will change their position, personality or
internal identity to avoid arguments with the
narcissist.

*"though **shape shifting** is a form of survival, we are never to
be in a survival mode in a relationship."*

should shaming
\ [should • sham·ing] \

category:

an abuse technique where the narcissist uses the
word "should" as a form of abuse to devalue and
shame the victim.

*"examples of **should shaming** include: "You should not have
done that." "You should not have said that."*

silent rule book
\ [siilent • rule·book] \

category:

the unspoken rules that govern the narcissistic
relationship, where the victim learns how to
behave via a system of punishment and reward.

*"in every narcissistic relationship you learn the unspoken
rules by trial and error; so though there is no an actual book
you are handed, there is a **silent rule book** you must learn to
survive."*

silent treatment
category: 💣※

\ [silent ◆ treat·ment] \

a period of non-responsiveness when the narcissist disappears and/or ignores their partner as if he or she doesn't exist.

*"the narcissist implements the **silent treatment** as a form of punishment and narcissistic conditioning. It is one of the most crazy-making abuses of the narcissist."*

sld friends
category: ☹

\ [sld ◆ friends] \

SLD is the acronym for Self-Love Deficiency. A SLD friend is a person the survivor of narcissistic abuse had or made while suffering under narcissistic abuse and who they lost once they began the recovery journey. Research shows that once a victim enters recovery, they will lose 70% - 80% of their friendship circle.

*"**sld friends** are "friends" who need the victim to be "ill" to enjoy the benefits of the relationship.*

smear campaign
category: 💣※

\ [smear ◆ camp·aign] \

a calculated public defamation campaign where the narcissist discredits the victim to their family or social sphere.

*"the purpose of the **smear campaign** is for the narcissist to receive sympathy, avoid accountability or punish their target because of a narcissistic injury."*

somatic narcissist

category:

\ [so·ma·tic ◆ nar·ci·ssist] \

a narcissist who is fixated on their body and appearance. They are often seductive and are pathological.

*"the problem with being in a relationship with a **somatic narcissist** is that both people in the relationship are in love with the same person."*

sociopath

category:

\ [so·cio·path] \

a marker on the narcissistic spectrum that describes a person with narcissistic personality disorder, only worse. People with sociopathy are believed to have gotten the condition from environment rather than biology, but unlike those with psychopathy their behaviors are more spontaneous than calculated.

*"a person with sociopathy, aka a **sociopath**, has a lack of a conscience or remorse as well as a high desire and ability to manipulate and deceive."*

soul trauma
category: ☹

\ [soul • trau·ma] \

the post trauma result a victim has after leaving a narcissistic relationship, where they understand the depth of abuse they survived at an emotional, spiritual and psychological level.

"narcissistic abuse creates not just mental trauma or physical trauma, it also creates soul trauma that takes years to heal from."

space pollution
category: 💣

\ [space • po·lu·tion] \

a control technique where the narcissist will control environments and extract fuel by acting out or misbehaving.

"the narcissist creates space pollution by pouting, shouting, demeaning, and ignoring his or her partner when they don't get her way."

space nazi
category: 💣

\ [space • na·zi] \

also known as space abuse it is a control technique where the narcissist controls space by taking over shared space or by intruding into the personal space of the victim.

"signs of a space nazi include:

A) controlling social space by putting limits on friendships and activities, screening calls, or prohibiting people to visit the home.

B) controlling intellectual space by constantly interrupting or arguing with the victim until he or she gives into exhaustion.

C) invading quiet time by talking when the victim wants to be alone or needs silence, especially when he or she needs to gather their thoughts.

D) invading privacy by demanding social activity details, past relationship details, opening emails, insisting on passcodes, and reading phone text.

E) invading sleep by interrupting sleep time with either selfish acts or needs, insisting the victim only services the children, or by waking the victim when the narcissist feels the need for him or her to be awake.

F) controlling personal space by monitoring or controlling the use of the bathroom, for example being required to leave the door open when using the facility, by monitoring the status of their closet or other personal space, or by ongoing pressure to have sex when the victim is not ready.

spectrum   category: ✿

\ [spec·trum] \
(see narcissistic spectrum)

sphere of influence   category: ✿
\ [sphere ◆ of ◆ in·flu·ence] \

a recovery tool where the survivor becomes
consciously aware of the power the narcissist
possesses to affect events, people and
developments of an individual or organization.

*"part of recovery sustainability requires the victim to clearly
see the **sphere of influence** the narcissist has and make a
game plan on how to protect themselves when exposed to
it."*

spiritual abuse   category:
\ [spir·it·ual ◆ a·buse] \

an abuse technique where the Bible, God, or any
form of religion is used to control or manipulate
another person into submission.

*"**spiritual abuse** slants scripture or any religious belief
towards the benefit of the narcissist and the disablement or
disempowerment of the victim."*

stonewalling   category: 💣✳

\ [stone·wall·ing] \

an abuse technique where the narcissist refuses
to engage in a conversation or provide information
on topics.

*"stonewalling happens when the narcissist does not want to
discuss something."*

spousal abandonment syndrome   category: ☹

\ [spous·al ♦ a·ban·don·ment] \

when one spouse leaves the marriage without any
warning and usually without having shown any
signs of unhappiness within the relationship.
(See discard)

*"he abruptly left the marriage and she suffered from **spousal
abonnement syndrome** for months."*

sun syndrome   category: ☹

\ [sun ♦ syn·drome] \

a syndrome where both the narcissist and the
victim believe that everyone in their environment
is supposed to revolve around the narcissist.

*"sun syndrome is most commonly seen in the narcissistic
family unit."*

survival mode   category: ☹
\ [sur·vi·val ✦ mode] \

a trauma response when the victim or target may go into unhealthy denial or avoidant behaviors simply to survive.

*"it is common to judge a person who is in **survival mode** as being ignorant."*

sustainable narcissism   category: ✿
\ [sus·tain·able ✦ nar·cis·sism] \

the term used to describe the two relational dynamics where narcissism can survive and thrive.

*"**sustainable narcissism** happens under two dynamics. 1) a narcissist and a narcissist and 2) a narcissist and an empath."*

syndrome   category: ✿
\ [syn·drome] \

a psychological term used to describe a set of signs and symptoms that cause physical, mental, emotional, and spiritual problems.

*"recovery requires us to look not only at the narcissist's **syndrome**, but ours as well."*

symptoms of narcissism   category: ⚙

\ [symp·tomes • of • nar·cis·sism] \

a psychological term used to describe a set of
signs and symptoms that cause physical, mental,
emotional, and spiritual problems.

*"symptoms of narcissism include but are not limited to: A
need for admiration, a lack of empathy, an exaggerated
sense of importance, persistent fantasies of increased
success, power, happiness, love, intelligence, or physical
appearance, a belief that they are so special that they
should only associate with other special people, a belief that
they should receive special attention, treatment, and gifts, a
tendency to take advantage of other people or situations to
fulfill their goals, lacking care, compassion, and empathy for
others, being envious of others and thinking that others are
envious of them, appearing arrogant, conceited, or self-
absorbed. A person only needs five of these qualities to
receive a diagnosis of NPD."*

T

target   category:

\ [tar·get] \

a person the narcissist identifies as a potential
primary fuel source and pursues with predator
instinct.

*"there are four types of people the narcissist **targets**. 1) a
person that has something the narcissist wants, including
money, power, position, or lifestyle. 2) those who have a
high caring temperament. 3) those who are empathetic. 4)
those who are wounded, weak and in need of love."*

time circus   category:

\ [time ◆ cir·cus] \

a control tactic the narcissist uses where he or
she is either a) not on time for appointments. b)
commits to something yet leaves the victim
waiting with no response or c), changes plans
arbitrarily.

*"the narcissist creates a **time circus** just to control and
demean the victim."*

tertiary fuel source
category:

\ [ter·ti·ary ♦ fuel♦ source] \

the third level or classification of people the
narcissist relies on for a "quick fix" supply.

*"tertiary fuel sources are people the narcissist can get fuel,
by either flattery or anger. Examples include grocery store
checkout clerks, waiters or waitresses, random drivers and
by-passers.*

the switch
category:

\ [the♦ switch] \

an abuse technique where the narcissist is nice
one minute and then cruel and mean the next.

"the switch is also known as Jekell Hyde behavior.'

toxic shame
category: ☹

\ [tox·ic ♦ shame] \

a trauma response where the victim suffers from
extreme negative self-evaluation that stems from
negative programming received in childhood and
relationships.

*"toxic shame is a condition that results from consistent
negative feedback from parents, teachers, or other adults.
A person who suffers from toxic shame believes their worth
is dependent on external variables and that they are
worthless or have no value without the validation of others."*

trauma bonds   category: ☹
\ [trau·ma • bonds] \

a form of misplaced loyalty where the victim of
narcissistic abuse is emotionally bonded to the
abuser and therefore finds themselves unable to
leave an unhealthy or dangerous relationship.
*"a **trauma bond** victim remains loyal to a fault, even if the
narcissist has repeatedly betrayed them."*

triangulation   category:
\ [tri·ang·u·la·tion] \

the the act of using a third party in a conflict to
make the narcissist appear "right", or to do the
narcissist's dirty work.
*"**triangulation** happens when a narcissist provokes rivalry and
jealousy between people."*

true self   category: ✿
\ [true • self] \

the authentic self.
*"the **true self** is discovered by a combination of our thoughts,
beliefs, and what is right and good for us."*

trauma memory   category: ☹
\ [trau·ma ♦ mem·or·y] \

a trauma memory that is stored in the limbic
system part of the brain that can or cannot be
recalled.
*"when triggered, **trauma memories** can prompt five
emotions: anxiety, despair, depression, pain and rage. These
five emotions are symbolic of CPTSD."*

trip zone   category: 💣⁕
\ [trip ♦ zone] \

a chronic state of confusion and panic where the
victim feels they cannot catch their breath or get
traction beneath their emotional feet.
*"the purpose of the narcissistic **trip zone** is to keep the
victim in a spin, which in turn provides a constant fuel
source for the narcissist."*

turds wrapped in gold syndrome   category: 💣⁕
\ [turds♦ wrapped♦ in ♦ gold ♦ syn·drome] \
(see couching)

types of narcissism   category: ✿
\ [types ♦ of ♦ nar·ci·ss·ism] \
in recovery, it is the various types of narcissism
that include Cerebral, Classic, Covert, Communal,

Delusional, Inverted, Malignant, Overt, Sadistic, Somatic and Vulnerable (See individual definitions for details)

*"many narcissist can have multiple **types of narcissism**."*

U

underwear drawer rule
category:

\ [un·der·wear ◆ drawer ◆ rule] \

a recovery tool that reminds the survivor that he or she has the right to certain privacies, even within a relationship.

*"no matter how much we love a person, we all have a right to or own **underwear drawer**.*

unmasking
category:

\ [un·mask·ing] \

a term used that describes when the false self of the narcissist is failing and those around are seeing him or her for what they really are.

*"**unmasking** happens when the narcissist removes their external mask and shows their target who they really are."*

unpredictable response
category:

\ [un·pre·dic·ta·ble ◆ re·sponse] \

a control technique the narcissist uses where for no apparent reason, dramatic and drastic mood swings, emotional outbursts or inconsistent responses happen.

*"the shocking mood swings and **unpredictable responses** ended up being a control tactic of the narcissist."*

unresolved pain   category:
\ [un·re·solved ✦ pain] \

pain that has not been delt with that is causing off-spring pain and trauma.

*"the challenge with trauma recovery is that the victim must work on both the existing pain and the **unresolved pain** at the same time."*

usurping   category:
\ [u·surp·ing] \

a control technique the narcissist uses when they take over their victims, rights, space, accomplishments, or position.

*"a narcissist does not walk into a room. They **usurp** the room."*

V

the veil
category:
\ [the ◆ veil] \

a term coined by Lisa Romano used to describe the
emotional blindness the victim of abuse lives
"behind" when she is unaware of the trauma and
abuses of the narcissist.
"it took her years to finally emerge from behind **the veil** *that
kept her blind."*

victim-blaming
category:
\ [vic·tim ◆ blam·ing] \

the act of blaming or partially blaming the victim for
the act of harm that has befallen him or her.
"the narcissist had the nerve to **victim blame** *her for the
assault he perpetrated."*

victim card
category:
\ [vic·tim ◆ card] \

a technique the narcissist uses when they attempt
to gain sympathy from others, with the ultimate
ulterior motive of excusing their abusive
behavior. They may blame it on something
negative in their past, a "bad childhood," a broken

heart, a lost love, a father that was never there or something else, or all of the above.

*"the narcissist pulled the **victim card** to avoid accountability."*

verbal abuse   category:
\ [ver·bal ✦ a·buse] \

when the narcissist uses words to putdown, humiliate, or weaken the self-esteem of the partner.

*"**verbal abuse** is identified by the misuse of words specifically name-calling, verbal assaulting, blaming, shaming, berating, belittling, criticizing, screaming, silent treatment, sarcasm, and humiliation."*

vibrational set point   category: ✿
\ [vi·bra·tion·al ✦ set·point] \

the level that we are vibrating at today, that will attract more of the same.

*"to heal, we must change our **vibrational set** point so we attract new and better things into our life."*

vulnerable narcissism   category:
\ [vul·ner·able ✦ nar·ci·ssi·sm] \

also known as covert narcissism and introverted narcissism, this is a subtype of narcissistic personality disorder that presents as a pervasive, maladaptive, and inflexible sensitivity to criticism and failure.

*"the **vulnerable narcissist** can manifest as part of the vulnerable dark triad."*

W

walking on egg shells
category:

\ [walk·ing ✦ on ✦ egg ✦ shells] \

a term used in the classic cycle of abuse when the victim is in the Tension Building Phase and they feel they are tip-toeing around the narcissist as to not activate or instigate a fight.

*"the victim was constantly **walking on egg-shells**, never being able to express her true self."*

weaponizing
category:

\ [wea·pon·i·zing] \

when the narcissist uses the victim's weaknesses, friends, or circumstances as weapons to harm them.

*"the narcissist knew that the mother of his children suffered from anxiety and as a way to control, he **weaponized** her condition by threatening take the children from her."*

wife abandonment syndrome
category:

\ [wife ✦ a·ban·don·ment ✦ syn·drome] \

(see spousal abandonment syndrome)

white knight narcissist

category:

\ [white ◆ knight ◆ nar·ci·ssit] \

a narcissist who is a combination of the covert
and overt narcissist. Specifically, they possess an
exaggerated self–importance, entitlement,
arrogance, need for admiration, lack of empathy
and exploitive behaviors of others, but as they
know people do not "like" this, they hide those
characteristics from others, making them a covert
narcissist. What differentiates them from the
covert narcissist is the way they get their fuel,
which is via altruism. (i.e., volunteering, being a
deacon at the church, run and fund programs to
serve communities, make large donations to
charity, lead non–profits, offer to help others
move, do yard work or other home projects),
where they receive fuel for their "gifts of good."

*"though she felt something was wrong, she did not
recognize for years that he was narcissist because he was a
white knight narcissist."*

withholding ◆

\ [with·holding] \

a technique the narcissist uses to put the victim
into deprivation. Examples of withholding include:
withholding finances, where one partner withholds
money from the other, leaving the one partner

unable to provide for their basic needs. Withholding material resources, where the victim cannot maintain a personal existence or well-being. Withholding sex from an intimate relationship, and and withholding love, communication and attention from the victim.

*"the trauma caused by the **withholding** was worse than the verbal assaults."*

wood peckering 💣✳
\ [wood ✦ peck·er·ing] \

an abuse technique where the narcissist will relentlessly poke and prod at the victim until they find the victim's tender spot and he or she will be brought to tears or anguish. The purpose of wood peckering is to extract fuel.

*"most victims breakdown because of the relentless **wood peckering** of the narcissist that chips away at their sanity."*

word salad 💣✳
\ [word ✦ salad] \

1) a mix of words that are thrown together with no coherence or structure. 2) Circular language tactics that the narcissist uses to ensure that conversations with others never have satisfactory resolutions or continued confusion for the other party. Word salad

includes projection, stonewalling, blame shifting
sympathy ploys, bringing up something the partner
did, bringing up unrelated issues, starting the
conversation over, using terms, arguments, or
techniques they've heard about yet don't really
understand, all while thinking that they are being
rational, reasonable, or correct. Listeners
find narcissistic word salad extremely frustrating
because the narcissist is using circular reasoning,
outright lies, <u>denial</u>, or mischaracterizations of
past events to avoid being wrong or having to
take responsibility for something. Meanwhile, in
reality, what they're saying is simply an
incoherent rant or an amalgamation of logical and
argumentation fallacies, factual errors, or pure
nonsense (as in something that literally makes no
sense).

*"**word salad(ing)** is one of the techniques the narcissist uses
to exhaust their victims."*

PART 3

Self-Assessment

The following pages are an at-a-glance checklist that will help you identify how much narcissistic abuse you have endured, how many trauma wounds you have, and how much recovery you have experienced. Check that which applies to you.

NARCISSISTIC ABUSE

Check the narcissistic abuses you have experienced.

[ ] abuse

[ ] abuse amnesia

[ ] abuse by proxy

[ ] abuse cycle

[ ] abuse tactics

[ ] abusive expectations

[ ] abusive spending

[ ] adored to abhorred

[ ] adult temper tantrum

[ ] altruistic narcissists

[ ] ambient abuse

[ ] anti-social personality disorder (ASPD)

[ ] arguing in bad faith

[ ] assigning responsibility

[ ] assigning status

[ ] baiting

[ ] bait and switch

[ ] battles without resolution

[ ] benign return

[ ] bidding

[ ] big / bigger syndrome

[ ] black-and-white thinking

[ ] black cloud syndrome

[ ] blame shifting

[ ] body language abuse

[ ] boiling frog syndrome

[ ] boundary push(es)

[ ] brainwashing

[ ] branding

[ ] bubble living

[ ] burdening

[ ] cerebral narcissist

[ ] character assassination

[ ] chess syndrome

[ ] circular argument

[ ] classic narcissist

NARCISSISTIC ABUSE, continued

[ ] cluster b personality disorder

[ ] cognitive empathy

[ ] communal narcissist

[ ] constant chaos

[ ] constant criticism

[ ] controlling behaviors

[ ] couching

[ ] covert narcissist

[ ] covert love bombing by-proxy

[ ] crazymaking

[ ] crumbs

[ ] cycle of abuse

[ ] dark tetrad

[ ] defining motive

[ ] defining reality

[ ] defining truth

[ ] deflecting

[ ] delusional narcissist

[ ] de-masking

[ ] devaluation phase

[ ] director of judgement

[ ] discard

[ ] distancing

[ ] divide and conquer

[ ] dog whistling

[ ] domestic violence

[ ] domination

[ ] dosing

[ ] double binding

[ ] double standards

[ ] drama triangle

[ ] drilling for fuel

[ ] ego-syntonic

[ ] emotional abuse

[ ] emotional blackmail

[ ] emotional face blindness

[ ] emotional infection

[ ] emotional manipulation

[ ] emotional neglect

NARCISSISTIC ABUSE, continued

[ ] emotional terrorist

[ ] emotional terrorism

[ ] emotional vampire

[ ] empathy deficient

[ ] empty husk

[ ] episodic

[ ] explosive disorder

[ ] ex-recycling

[ ] fake empathy

[ ] false flattery

[ ] false self

[ ] fauxpology

[ ] fear bombing

[ ] fictional character

[ ] final discard

[ ] financial abuse

[ ] fights over nothing

[ ] fleas

[ ] flying monkeys

[ ] hyper-vigilance

[ ] fuel reaction

[ ] fuel / fuel source

[ ] future faking

[ ] gaslighting

[ ] glass with holes

[ ] golden child

[ ] golden period

[ ] good narc - bad narc

[ ] grandiose narcissist

[ ] grandstanding

[ ] grand finale

[ ] granting

[ ] grooming

[ ] grooming phase

[ ] harem

[ ] honeymoon period

[ ] follow-up hoover

[ ] hurt to rescue

[ ] hyper emotions

[ ] initial grand hoover

NARCISSISTIC ABUSE, continued

[ ] Idealization

[ ] idealization phase one

[ ] identify theft

[ ] integrating behavior

[ ] intellectual empathy

[ ] intermittent reinforcement

[ ] intermittent explosive disorder

[ ] invisible child

[ ] invalidation

[ ] invert narcissist

[ ] irritable male syndrome

[ ] isolation

[ ] love bombing

[ ] madonna complex

[ ] malign return

[ ] malignant narcissist

[ ] marginalizing

[ ] mask slipping

[ ] mask / masking

[ ] mascot

[ ] mask / masking

[ ] mean and sweet cycle

[ ] megalomaniac

[ ] mental disorder

[ ] mental abuse

[ ] misdirected anger

[ ] minimalizing

[ ] mirroring

[ ] misdirected anger

[ ] moving the goal post

[ ] moving the start line

[ ] mr / ms breathy

[ ] mr / ms long face

[ ] mr / ms opposite

[ ] my way or the highway syndrome

[ ] mythical thinking

[ ] narcanese

NARCISSISTIC ABUSE, continued

[ ] narcissist

[ ] narcissistic brain damage

[ ] narcissistic branding

[ ] narcissistic bubble

[ ] narcissistic collapse

[ ] narcissistic consumption

[ ] narcissistic conditioning

[ ] narcissistic despair cycle

[ ] narcissistic environment

[ ] narcissistic envy

[ ] narcissistic family system

[ ] narcissistic filter

[ ] narcissistic injury

[ ] narcissistic mind reading

[ ] narcissistic nit-picking

[ ] narcissistic perfectionism

[ ] narcissistic projection

[ ] narcissistic rage

[ ] narcissistic storms

[ ] narcissistic supply

[ ] narcissistic view finder

[ ] narkie-ville

[ ] neglect

[ ] nice to nasty cycle

[ ] non-productive arguments

[ ] non-validation

[ ] object constancy

[ ] overt narcissist

[ ] parasite

[ ] parental alienation syndrome

[ ] parentification

[ ] pathological lying

[ ] pawn

[ ] pedestal

[ ] physical abuse

[ ] playbook

[ ] pitch forking

[ ] plausible denial

[ ] projection

NARCISSISTIC ABUSE, continued

[ ] primary resource   [ ] shame dumping

[ ] private shaming   [ ] shape shifting

[ ] psychic virus   [ ] should shaming

[ ] psychopath   [ ] silent rule book

[ ] public shaming   [ ] silent treatment

[ ] rage disorder   [ ] sld friends

[ ] reactive anger   [ ] smear campaign

[ ] recharge   [ ] somatic narcissist

[ ] reality warping   [ ] sociopath

[ ] redefining   [ ] space pollution

[ ] rumination   [ ] space nazi

[ ] sadistic narcissist   [ ] spiritual abuse

[ ] scapegoat   [ ] stonewalling

[ ] scorecard   [ ] target

[ ] segmented love   [ ] time circus

[ ] secondary resource   [ ] tertiary fuel source

[ ] secret shaming   [ ] the switch

[ ] sexual harassment

NARCISSISTIC ABUSE, continued

[ ] triangulation   [ ] sanctuary wounds

[ ] trip zone   [ ] scapegoat

[ ] turds wrapped in gold syndrome

[ ] unmasking   [ ] segmented love

[ ] unpredictable response

[ ] unresolved pain   [ ] self-love deficiency disorder

[ ] usurping   [ ] soul trauma   L

[ ] victim-blaming   [ ] spousal abandonment

[ ] victim card   syndrome

[ ] verbal abuse   [ ] sun syndrome

[ ] vulnerable narcissism   [ ] survival mode

[ ] weaponizing   [ ] toxic shame

[ ] white knight narcissist [ ] trauma bonds

[ ] withholding   [ ] trauma memory

[ ] wood puckering   [ ] the veil

[ ] word salad   [ ] walking on egg shells

[ ] resigned passiveness   ☹

[ ] respite

NARCISSISTIC TRAUMA WOUND

Check the narcissistic trauma wounds you have / had

[ ] abuse amnesia   [ ] constant analysis

[ ] acute stress response   [ ] contagious insanity

[ ] aftershock   [ ] compassion fatigue

[ ] abandoned child syndrome

[ ] belief conflicts   [ ] cptsd

[ ] black-and-white thinking   [ ] denial

[ ] black cloud syndrome   [ ] detectiving

[ ] boiling frog syndrome   [ ] diminished identity

[ ] brainwashing   [ ] dissociative amnesia

[ ] branding   [ ] emotional dissonance

[ ] broken heart syndrome   [ ] emotional flashback

[ ] broken record syndrome   [ ] emotional homelessness

[ ] bubble living   [ ] emotional thinking

[ ] burnout dissociation   [ ] emotional threshold

[ ] chess syndrome   [ ] enabler engaging

[ ] cluster b personality   [ ] enmeshment

[ ] closure fog   [ ] erased syndrome

[ ] co-dependency   [ ] fearland citizenship

[ ] cognitive dissonance   [ ] fixed condition

NARCISSISTIC TRAUMA WOUND, con't.
☹

[ ] flashback   [ ] madonna complex

[ ] fog   [ ] mascot

[ ] golden child   [ ] misdirected anger

[ ] golden period   [ ] narcissistic abuse syndrome

[ ] harem   [ ] narcissistic branding

[ ] head living   [ ] narcissistic conditioning

[ ] hyper emotions   [ ] narcissistic despair cycle

[ ] idealization   [ ] narcissistic environment

[ ] idealization phase one   [ ] narcissistic fatigue

[ ] identify shift   [ ] lost child syndrome

[ ] impending doom   [ ] narcissistic induced fear

[ ] inner critic   [ ] narcissistic nit-picking

[ ] integrating behavior   [ ] narcissistic personality disorder

[ ] invisible child   [ ] narcissistic victim syndrome

[ ] invisible self   [ ] normalizing

[ ] jokasti syndrome (recipient of)

[ ] jekyll hyde syndrome (recipient of)

[ ] learned helplessness   [ ] out of integrity

[ ] linen cupboard syndrome [ ] pathological critic

[ ] love addiction   [ ] post abuse despair syndrome

NARCISSISTIC TRAUMA RECOVERY
☼

Check the recovery you have experienced

[ ] acons

[ ] anticipated losses

[ ] awakening

[ ] api technique

[ ] belief system

[ ] birthrights

[ ] boundaries

[ ] boundary push-backs

[ ] core identity

[ ] deal breakers

[ ] do-overs

[ ] dsm (knowledge of)

[ ] emotional bandwidth

[ ] emotional boundaries

[ ] emotional home base

[ ] emotional neutral

[ ] empath

[ ] fight, flight, freeze or fawn

[ ] first voice

[ ] grey rock

[ ] healthy narcissism

[ ] heart living

[ ] individuation

[ ] internal guidance system

[ ] is factor

[ ] low contact

[ ] narcanese (able to hear it)

[ ] narcissistic abuse cycle

[ ] narcissistic spectrum (knowledge of)

[ ] narcissistic tendencies (knowledge of)

[ ] no contact

[ ] non-negotiables

[ ] narkie-ville   (knowledge of)

[ ] observe don't absorb system

[ ] personality disorder (knowledge of)

[ ] pink cloud syndrome

[ ] poop in your soup

NARCISSISTIC TRAUMA RECOVERY

☼

[ ] prediction and preparation   [ ] symptoms of narcissism

[ ] present time living   [ ] true self

[ ] predictive awareness   [ ] types of narcissism

[ ] reciprocity   [ ] underwear drawer rule

[ ] reality check   [ ] vibrational set point

[ ] resolution

[ ] righteous anger

[ ] safe and sacred place

[ ] self-esteem

[ ] self-love

[ ] self-love foundation

[ ] self-partnering

[ ] self-regulating

[ ] self-soothing

[ ] self-care

[ ] self-rescue

[ ] spectrum

[ ] sphere of influence

[ ] sustainable narcissism

[ ] syndrome

PART 4

Recovery

It is said that once you survive a narcissistic relationship, you are never the same. Meaning, the person you once were, is nowhere to be found. The innocence and trust you had in mankind are both annihilated. Your understanding of love has been destroyed. Even your interpretation of self has been turned into something you no longer recognize. That is why recovery from narcissistic abuse trauma must be a non-negotiable.

In 1996, after I found my initial way out of Narkie-ville, (see my book "The Courage to Say No More) I started The WIN Foundation®, a 501-C3, non-profit outreach that specializes in abuse recovery. My passion for the foundation was to make healing from

abuse trauma easily available and affordable, which
was something not available to me when I began my
recovery.

Our cornerstone program at the foundation is called
Reclaiming Me (the Journey from Narcissistic Abuse
Trauma to Self-Love). It is a program that
specializes in narcissistic abuse recovery and to
date, we have helped tens of thousands of women
reclaim their life after narcissistic trauma.

Reclaiming Me is presented in 6 modules, where over
12 months, or 48 classes, our attendees are educated
on narcissism, narcissistic abuse, narcissistic abuse
trauma, and of course the road to narcissistic abuse
recovery.

What makes this program unique is that recovery
through the Reclaiming Me program has one primary
goal. That is to build a steely foundation of self-love
under your emotional feet.

In more clinical words, Reclaiming Me is focused on
healing a condition called Self-Love Deficiency
Disorder. This strategy is extremely important for
sustainable healing because research shows that

Self–Love Deficiency Disorder is the precursor to narcissistic abuse. Therefore, where self–love is, narcissistic abuse cannot be.

Every week in the Reclaiming Me program we focus on gaining the tools, skills, and mindsets to align our self to self–love. This then, dis–aligns us with narcissism, which in turn empowers us to break the physical, emotional and spiritual bonds that keep us tethered to narcissistic abuse.

Reclaiming Me, which I believe is an antidote to narcissist abuse, is a program that is filled with wisdom, tools, Memos from Self–Love Normal Land®, support, answers, and a clear roadmap that will teach you how to reclaim your life after narcissistic abuse.

Details on the Reclaiming Me program are outlined on the following pages. We meet every week in a live classroom, or if you prefer, you can also access the program privately online.

I invite you to attend a class as my guest. There is a QR code below that will connect you directly to a link for a complimentary pass, where our team is waiting to take your hand and help you too reclaim your life after narcissistic abuse.

Until we meet in person···

Dr. Tracy
@drtracykemble
@reclaimingmewithdrtracy
www.DrTracy.tv

RECLAIMING ME

(The Journey from Narcissistic Abuse to Self-Love)

JOIN ME AS MY GUEST

RECLAIMING ME
(The Journey from Narcissistic Abuse to Self-Love)

MODULE 1:
SELF-L♡VE AND NARCISSISM
(What is This?!)

1.1 FROM SELF-LOVE DEFICIENCY TO SELF-LOVE
Why Self-Love is the Antidote to Narcissistic. Abuse

1.2 FROM "WHAT IS THIS?!" TO SELF-LOVE
Understanding the various types of abuse

1.3 FROM FUEL SOURCE TO SELF-LOVE
Understanding What Is Narcissistic Abuse

1.4 FROM NARCISSISTIC ABUSE TO SELF-LOVE
Understanding Narcissistic Abuse Syndrome

1.5 FROM LOST TO SELF-LOVE
Finding Your Internal GPS

MODULE 2:
THE BREAKDOWN ROADMAP
(What Happened to Me?)

2.1 FROM FEAR TO SELF-LOVE
Understanding Why They Manipulate

2.2 FROM BRAIN WASHED TO SELF-LOVE
Understanding Narcissistic Abuse Conditioning

2.3 FROM DEPRESSION TO SELF-LOVE
Understanding Narcissistic induced Depression

2.4 FROM EMOTIONAL BLUR TO SELF-LOVE
Finding Your Truth When the Narcissist Gaslights

2.5 FROM CONFUSION TO SELF-LOVE
Healing from Cognitive Dissonance & Rumination

2.6 FROM INVISIBLE TO SELF-LOVE
Understanding Narcissistic Identity Theft

2.7 FROM NARCISSISTIC FATIGUE TO SELF-LOVE
Narcissistic Fatigue & Transformational pain

2.8 FROM NARCISSISTIC PERFECTION TO SELF-LOVE
Healing from Abusive Expectations

2.9 FROM BLAME GAME TO SELF-LOVE
Healing from Narcissistic Projection

2.10 FROM SEXUAL BETRAYAL TO SELF-LOVE
Healing from Sexual Betrayal

2.11 FROM REACTIVE ANGER TO SELF-LOVE
Understanding Reactive & Righteous Anger

MODULE 3:
LOVE AND THE NARCISSIST
(Breaking the Root Addiction)

3.1 WOUNDED EMPATH TO SELF-LOVE
Why Narcissists Choose Us

3.2 FROM FROM THE DISCARD TO SELF-LOVE
Why the Step Away and Repeat

3.3 FROM CODEPENDENCE TO SELF-LOVE
Why we Choose the Narcissist

3.4 FROM LOVE ADDICTION TO SELF-LOVE
Understanding Why we Go Back for More

3.5 FROM TRAUMA BOND TO SELF-LOVE
Understanding Why we Stay

3.6 FROM SPIRITUALLY BONDED TO SELF-LOVE
Breaking the Tether

3.7 FROM LOVE BOMBING TO SELF-LOVE
Learning to use the Narcissist's Kryptonite

3.8 FROM BOUNDARY-LESS TO SELF-LOVE
Learning to use the Narcissist's Kryptonite

MODULE 4:
THE AFTERMATH OF NARCISSISTIC ABUSE
(Healing from CPTSD)

4.1 FROM CPTSD TO SELF-LOVE
Understanding the Trauma

4.2 FROM ABANDONMENT TO SELF-LOVE
Learning the Root of Narcissistic Abuse

4.3 FROM ANXIETY TO SELF-LOVE
Understanding Hypervigilance & Narcissism

4.4 FROM PERFECTIONISM TO SELF-LOVE
Healing the Inner Critic

4.5 FROM TOXI SHAME TO SELF-LOVE
Healing the Inner Bondage

4.6 FROM REPEAT TO SELF-LOVE
Understanding Aftershock

MODULE 5:

THE FAMILY AND THE NARCISSIST

(When No Contact is Not an Option

5.1 FROM PARENTLESS TO SELF-LOVE – PART I
Understanding Narcissistic Parents and Parenting

5.2 FROM ROUND 2 TO SELF-LOVE – PART 2
When Children Become the Narcissist

5.3 FROM CRAZY-COPARENTING TO SELF-LOVE
How to Save Yourself and Your Children

5.4 FROM STAYING TO SELF-LOVE
When Leaving is Not an Option

MODULE 6:
LOVE, THE FUTURE AND THE REBUILD
(Life After Narcissistic Abuse

6.1 FROM DIVORCED TO SELF-LOVE
Surviving the Divorce Process

6.2 FROM SMEARED TO SELF-LOVE
Surviving the Smear Campaign

6.3 FROM HOPELESS TO SELF-LOVE
Dreams, Choices, and processing Revenge

6.4 FROM UNFORGIVEABLE TO SELF-LOVE
Finding the Right Time to Forgive

6.5 FROM POWERLESS TO SELF-LOVE
Remembering Your Personal Power

6.6 FROM INVISIBLE TO SELF-LOVE
Keeping Your Joy in the Holidays

OTHER WORK BY DR. TRACY

Books (available on Amazon)

- The Courage to Say No More (Overcoming the Scars of Emotional Abuse

- How Not to Care What People Think

- Don't Touch My Tiara

Connect on Social Media to discover more!
@drtracykemble   @reclaimingmewithdrtracy

Made in the USA
Coppell, TX
04 March 2023

13679673R40115